Presented to

Michelle

From

Jessica

On this date

Christmas 2014

May the Lord keep watch
between you and me when we
are away from each other.
♡ Genesis 31:49

Sister, I ♡ you, Merry Christmas!

Missing

Jessica

Christmas 2014
May the Lord keep watch
between you and me when we
are away from each other.

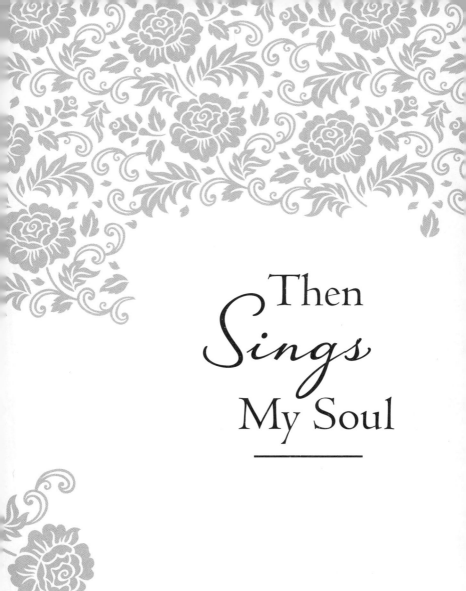

Then
Sings
My Soul

Then *Sings* My Soul

Devotions Inspired by
Ten Beloved Hymns

BARBOUR
PUBLISHING

© 2014 by Barbour Publishing, Inc.

Print ISBN 978-1-62416-881-9

eBook Editions:
Adobe Digital Edition (.epub) 978-1-63058-107-7
Kindle and MobiPocket Edition (.prc) 978-1-63058-108-4

Scripture quotations marked NIV are taken from the HOLY BIBLE, NEW INTERNATIONAL VERSION®. NIV®. Copyright © 1973, 1978, 1984, 2011 by Biblica, Inc.™ Used by permission. All rights reserved worldwide.

Scripture quotations marked NKJV are taken from the New King James Version®. Copyright © 1982 by Thomas Nelson, Inc. Used by permission. All rights reserved.

Scripture quotations marked NASB are taken from the New American Standard Bible, © 1960, 1962, 1963, 1968, 1971, 1972, 1973, 1975, 1977, 1995 by The Lockman Foundation. Used by permission.

Scripture quotations marked CEV are from the Contemporary English Version, Copyright © 1995 by American Bible Society. Used by permission.

Scripture quotations marked NLT are taken from the *Holy Bible*. New Living Translation copyright© 1996, 2004, 2007 by Tyndale House Foundation. Used by permission of Tyndale House Publishers, Inc. Carol Stream, Illinois 60188. All rights reserved.

Scripture quotations marked AMP are taken from the Amplified® Bible, © 1954, 1958, 1962, 1964, 1965, 1987 by The Lockman Foundation. Used by permission.

Scripture quotations marked ESV are from The Holy Bible, English Standard Version®, copyright © 2001 by Crossway Bibles, a publishing ministry of Good News Publishers. Used by permission. All rights reserved.

Scripture quotations marked MSG are from *THE MESSAGE*. Copyright © by Eugene H. Peterson 1993, 1994, 1995, 1996, 2000, 2001, 2002. Used by permission of NavPress Publishing Group.

Scripture quotations marked NCV are taken from the New Century Version of the Bible, copyright © 2005 by Thomas Nelson, Inc. Used by permission. All rights reserved.

Scripture quotations marked KJV are taken from the King James Version of the Bible.

Published by Barbour Publishing, Inc., P.O. Box 719, Uhrichsville, Ohio 44683, www.barbourbooks.com

Our mission is to publish and distribute inspirational products offering exceptional value and biblical encouragement to the masses.

Member of the
Evangelical Christian
Publishers Association

Printed in China.

Contents

Introduction

There's a reason the classic hymns have stood the test of time. The combination of powerful lyrics and a memorable tune—all directed to the glory of God—will keep people singing for decades, even centuries, after the song is written.

This devotional will challenge and encourage you with inspiration from ten timeless songs of faith:

- "To God Be the Glory"
- "Amazing Grace"
- "It Is Well with My Soul"
- "All Things Bright and Beautiful"
- "Blessed Assurance"
- "Sweet Hour of Prayer"
- "Count Your Blessings"
- "Great Is Thy Faithfulness"
- "Wonderful Words of Life"
- "What a Friend We Have in Jesus"

Each of the 150 brief, easy-to-read entries in this book is accompanied by an evocative prayer, memorable quotations, and powerful Bible promises. If you love the old hymns—or if you're just discovering them— *Then Sings My Soul* will certainly put a song in your heart!

To God Be the Glory

To God be the glory, great things He has done;
So loved He the world that He gave us His Son,
Who yielded His life an atonement for sin,
And opened the life gate that all may go in.

REFRAIN
Praise the Lord, praise the Lord,
Let the earth hear His voice!
Praise the Lord, praise the Lord,
Let the people rejoice!
O come to the Father, through Jesus the Son,
And give Him the glory, great things He has done.

O perfect redemption, the purchase of blood,
To every believer the promise of God;
The vilest offender who truly believes,
That moment from Jesus a pardon receives.

FANNY CROSBY, 1875

Fanny Crosby was one of the best-loved hymn writers of the nineteenth century, penning more than eight thousand hymns during her lifetime. Blinded at six weeks of age due to a medical error, she learned to view her disability as a blessing in disguise, allowed by a loving God to help her "see" heavenly things more clearly without the distractions of physical sight.

While in her forties, Fanny began writing hymns, the vast majority of which were published and well-received, including "Draw Me Nearer" and "Safe in the Arms of Jesus." She wrote "To God Be the Glory" in 1875, but it didn't become popular until 1954, when Billy Graham discovered it during a crusade in England and brought it back to America. There it was enthusiastically received and adopted as one of the standard hymns of the Billy Graham crusades.

Great Things He Has Done

Stand still, and consider the wondrous works of God.
JOB 37:14 KJV

There are plenty of things in this life to worry about. We face difficult decisions with lifelong consequences. There are health issues and finances to fret over, family responsibilities to juggle, and hectic schedules to meet. Our prayer lists overflow. With so much demanding our attention, it's easy to become discouraged. But however mountainous our problems appear, God is bigger. His blessings to us are innumerable. All we have to do is remember them.

Gaze up at the night sky, alight with moon and stars. Behold the intricate network of veins in a simple leaf. All of nature—from the tallest mountain to the tiniest living organism—was brought into existence by the great Creator's *"let there be. . . ."*

He who placed the sun and commanded it to shine by day also parted the seas for His people and fed them with bread from Heaven. By His power, a virgin gave birth to a Son. By His will, that Son died on a cross to restore mankind's lost innocence. His loving arms are stretched wide to receive the brokenhearted and His kiss of forgiveness removes our shameful guilt.

Truly the Lord is good! His mercies are new every morning. He showers us with good things and abundantly supplies our every need. No matter how difficult the journey becomes, let us never forget the works of Almighty God. Instead, let us cry with the psalmist: "Great is the LORD, and most worthy of praise" (Psalm 48:1).

Amazing Love

*For God so loved the world, that he gave his only
begotten Son, that whosoever believeth in
him should not perish, but have everlasting life.*
JOHN 3:16 KJV

Do we ever doubt God's love for us? We wouldn't be human if we didn't. Sometimes we pass through seasons of discouragement when it feels like *nobody* understands or cares. Such is the problem with feelings. Sky high today, plunging tomorrow.

God's Word reminds us that, no matter how we feel, nothing can separate us from His love. If we're uncertain of this, we have only to look at Calvary. Nothing but the fiercest, most sincere love could keep Jesus on the cross when it was in His power to call for rescue. His passion for our eternal souls demanded that He give Himself for our sins, not only to grant us everlasting life but also to make us joyful in this one.

God delights in our happiness. Such is the nature of His love. Unlike our human passions that burn with molten fervor in one season, then grow frigid with frost in the next, God's love is forever constant. Forged in the dawning of time, tested throughout the ages, written in stone, and sealed with blood, it is ours eternally.

Remember that in your times of loneliness, when friends are distant and family ties unravel, when hardships strike and griefs assail. The God who did not spare His only Son for your sake will never leave you. His love endures forever.

But God showed his great
love for us by sending
Christ to die for us
while we were still sinners.
ROMANS 5:8 NLT

God loves each of us as
if there were only one of us.
SAINT AUGUSTINE

Almighty Father, You are Lord of creation and
Lord of my life. You have blessed me in more
ways than I could ever recount. You give me
the strength to press on despite my trials.
Your courage enables me to do things that
I thought were impossible. I can never repay
Your goodness, dear Lord, but I can praise You.
And with my whole heart, I do so. Amen.

Yielding

Nothing brings more relief than surrendering our wills to God and allowing Him to mold us into the women He wants us to be. But doing so sounds much easier than it is. We have an enemy, and her name is Self.

Self demands to have her own way. She resists the authority of her husband, scorning the notion that God expects her to submit to a man. She sees a friend's counsel as interference. Parental advice seems meddlesome. The boss isn't fair, and the government is corrupt. She is attracted to others just like her, although she secretly detests them. When she is in control, our lives are miserable. Only by surrendering to God can we defeat her.

When we have yielded to our Savior, we delight in obeying Him. Though Self rises at every opportunity to reclaim her throne, we resist her, preferring the blessings of God to her spiteful charms. We recognize that submission to husbands, pastors, parents, workplace authority, and government (though it may indeed be corrupt!) is really submission to God.

If Self seems hard to defeat, we should journey to Calvary. There, we find the very portrait of submission. Though divine, Christ was still human. He didn't want to suffer and die. But He kept His self consecrated to His Father's will, knowing that doing so would earn the greatest triumph in the end.

And it did. We are the bounty of His submission.

The Life Gate

And it shall come to pass, that whosoever
shall call on the name of the Lord shall be saved.
ACTS 2:21 KJV

Regardless of race, regardless of education, regardless of financial status or family ancestry, anyone can have a relationship with Almighty God. The life gate was thrown wide open at Calvary, when Jesus declared with His final breath, "It is finished." At that moment, the curtain blocking the entrance into the Most Holy Place where God dwelt was torn in half. He who had been known only to the Jewish nation and their proselytes became available to *whosoever*.

Rather than conquering Rome and reestablishing Israel's kingdom as His kinsman hoped, Jesus set up a spiritual one. One so mighty that even the powers of hell can never destroy it. He welcomes His subjects from all walks of life, having paved the way for every man, woman, and child to enter. There's no need to prove lineages or perform painful rites. The costly entrance fee, far too high for anyone's purse, has already been paid. All the Lord requires is a heart willing to serve Him.

Have you passed through the life gate? Jesus bids everyone who is weary and thirsty to come. Shed your burdens and drink freely from the water of life. Let Him take your filthy rags and clothe you in the white robe of righteousness. His city is glorious and He eagerly waits to welcome you inside.

"I am the way, the truth, and the life.
No one can come to the Father except through me."
JOHN 14:6 NLT

No soul can be really at rest until it has given
up all dependence on everything else and has
been forced to depend on the Lord alone.
HANNAH WHITALL SMITH

Dear God, although I know that you have my best
interest at heart, it's not always easy to submit to
Your will. Sometimes You lead me to places that
I don't want to go and ask me to do things
that I don't want to do. When I find myself resisting
Your will, remind me of the sacrifice that Jesus made
and help me to be as selfless as He was. Amen.

Perfect Redemption

*But as many as received him, to them
gave he power to become the sons of God,
even to them that believe on his name.*
JOHN 1:12 KJV

Eve had it made. A peaceful home, a perfect relationship with her husband, and an intimate bond with God. But as soon as the serpent beguiled her to eat the forbidden fruit, everything changed. Her disobedience brought guilt and shame. Suddenly, there was strife in her marriage, and for the first time ever, she was afraid of God. The peaceful paradise she had enjoyed was forever lost, not just to her and Adam, but to every human being who came afterward.

Jesus came to restore all that was stolen by the Deceiver on that fateful day. His sacrifice broke the curse of sin and made it possible for us to have a relationship with God once again. With our guilty stains washed away and our spiritual innocence restored, we can enjoy the same peace that the first humans experienced in Eden.

Christ's redemption is complete and powerful. When hearts are surrendered to Him, wounded relationships, broken marriages, and fragmented homes can all be restored. Though tremors from the first shock of sin are still felt in our fallen world, we can be separated from it. Our mortal bodies are weak, and we are affected by human emotions, yet our hearts can remain morally pure. Not by our own strength or might, but by the awesome power of the cross.

The Purchase of Blood

Bless the LORD, O my soul, and forget not all his benefits:
who forgiveth all thine iniquities; who healeth all thy diseases;
who redeemeth thy life from destruction;
who crowneth thee with lovingkindness and tender mercies.
PSALM 103:2–4 KJV

We often live beneath our privileges. We learn to put up with what's wrong in our lives, rather than asking God to make it right. Instead of pressing Him for what we need, we get accustomed to our lack. But Christ didn't shed His blood so that we could remain defeated. He purchased everything that our souls crave. All we have to do is ask Him for it.

Is your soul burdened with the guilt of sin? Jesus was wounded for our transgressions. When we repent of our wickedness, His kiss of forgiveness drives away all condemnation. Do you find yourself anxious and fretful? He was chastised for our peace. Is your heart broken by pain and loss? By the Savior's stripes we are healed.

Christ bore our grief and carried our sorrows. He was oppressed and afflicted, endured heavy temptation, was hungry and homeless and despised by the very ones He came to deliver. Even as His flesh recoiled from the horror of the cross, His great love compelled Him to endure it. The blood that dripped from His crowned forehead and spilled from His wounded side is a fountain that still flows today.

There is a Balm in Gilead. It's right at your fingertips. Reach out and touch Him.

He sent redemption to his people;
he has commanded his covenant forever.
Holy and awesome is his name!
PSALM 111:9 ESV

I thought I could have leaped from earth
to heaven at one spring when I first saw
my sins drowned in the Redeemer's blood.
CHARLES H. SPURGEON

Lord, You see my past and the terrible things I've done.
You know the people I've hurt and those who have hurt me.
I am haunted by my guilt. Deliver me from my wickedness,
Lord. Rescue me from the pit that I have dug for myself.
You said that You would not despise a broken and contrite heart,
Lord, so I bring You mine. Amen.

Mercy's Pardon

Be ye therefore merciful,
as your Father also is merciful.
LUKE 6:36 KJV

It's not always easy to forgive. Simple misunderstandings can be brushed off, and petty grievances can be reconciled, but some wounds are deep and difficult to heal. Try as we might to forget, painful memories fade slowly. Scenes replay, transporting us back to the moment of injury. We agonize over our own role in the offense, wondering what we might have said or done differently to avoid the whole mess. If left untreated, our hearts can become joyless and miserable, a fertile breeding ground for bitterness and even hatred.

Jesus is our example of forgiveness. He was insulted and slandered, ridiculed by His family members, and betrayed by one of His closest friends. He was beaten and spat upon, falsely accused, and condemned to die. Yet, even at the height of His agony, Christ said of the jeering crowd, "Father forgive them, they know not what they do." He had mercy on their pitiful human hearts and gave up His right to take vengeance.

Our Savior bids us to walk in His footsteps. His sacrifice reminds us that no matter how grievous the injury, we can find grace to forgive. When we place the injustice—and the one who inflicted it—in God's hands, we begin the healing process. Our hearts do not have to grow brittle with resentment. He who graciously forgave our own trespasses can give us the strength to bestow that same mercy on others.

Promises

---

*Whereby are given unto us exceeding
great and precious promises. . .*
2 PETER 1:4 KJV

Making promises is one thing. Keeping them is another. Despite good intentions, human vows are unreliable at best. But heaven and earth will pass away before one of God's words will fail. Our confidence in His promises gives comfort and courage like nothing else can.

An uncertain future isn't as troubling when we remember Jeremiah 29:11. If we're struggling with finances, we have the promise from Philippians 4:19 that God will supply all of our needs. In seasons of temptation, we can lean on 1 Corinthians 10:13 and look for our way of escape. If we lack wisdom, James 1:5 tells us to ask God for it. When it seems that our entire life is crumbling to dust at our feet, we can take courage in knowing, according to Romans 8:28, that all things work together for our good.

As wonderful as these promises are, nothing gives more hope than the one found in 1 Corinthians 2:9 (KJV). "Eye hath not seen, nor ear heard, neither have entered into the heart of man, the things which God hath prepared for them that love Him." Eternal life purchased at Calvary for all the redeemed, is the reward for following Christ to the very end. Tuck this jewel of hope away for those seasons of difficulty when it seems your feet can't take another step. Heaven will be worth it all. God promised it.

And be ye kind one to another,
tenderhearted, forgiving one another, even as
God for Christ's sake hath forgiven you.
EPHESIANS 4:32 KJV

I have always found that mercy
bears richer fruits than strict justice.
ABRAHAM LINCOLN

Lord, it is not Your will for me to harbor resentment toward
those who have wronged me. I want to obey You in all things,
and Your Word teaches me to forgive others just as You have
forgiven me. Some things are hard to let go of, Lord. For
my own soul's sake, help me to place all that troubles me in
Your hands and let Your touch heal my wounds. Amen.

True Belief

*Herein is my Father glorified, that ye
bear much fruit; so shall ye be my disciples.*
JOHN 15:8 KJV

It's easier to believe than to follow, to read the Bible than obey
it, to possess faith than to act on it. But belief without deeds is
useless. God gets no glory out of an empty profession. When we call
ourselves Christians, our actions should mirror our Master's.

There were plenty of people who believed in Jesus when He
walked the shores of Galilee, but few who gave up everything to
follow Him. Many were offended by His preaching because He
challenged motives as well as deeds. Though compassionate and
merciful, He wasn't afraid to proclaim judgment. He commanded
repentance and told people to go and sin no more.

In our lukewarm age, it's easy to be a lazy believer. Temptations
are strong and the flesh is weak. When people get on our nerves or
traffic is frustrating, we may feel justified in venting a few muttered
curses. If telling the truth isn't convenient, we might allow for a little
massaging of the facts. But when we choose to disobey God's Word,
we give nonbelievers the impression that Christianity is just another
powerless religion. When we stand for what's right and refuse to
compromise our values, we become a beacon of righteousness that
lifts up the One who enables us to do so.

Actions speak louder than words. What do yours say? Are you a
true believer?

Gathering Wisdom

All scripture is given by inspiration of God, and is profitable for doctrine, for reproof, for correction, for instruction in righteousness.
2 TIMOTHY 3:16 KJV

Regardless of how the Bible is viewed by an unbelieving world, true Christians understand that it is God's personal message to us. The stories may have taken place thousands of years ago, but the precepts hold true today. Villains and heroes from both testaments teach us valuable lessons about the follies of disobedience and the reward of faithfulness.

God's Word is alive. Though penned centuries ago by faithful writers, His Spirit witnesses to our hearts that what we read is true. When we obey that revealed Word, we grow in grace and wisdom. Just as the Israelites gathered manna each morning in the wilderness, so we should gather the nourishing bread of heaven. Our physical bodies grow weak from lack of food, and the same is true of our souls. Every Christian wants to grow and mature, but it will never happen unless we consistently feed on God's Word.

Taking the time to gather our soul's manna requires effort. The cares of life will rob every minute of our day, if we let them. But when we esteem the Word of God more than our necessary food (Job 23:12), we're willing to do whatever it takes. Have you read the Bible today? If not, take a few minutes to search the scriptures and see what the Lord has especially for you.

This is what the LORD says— your Redeemer, the Holy One of Israel: "I am the LORD your God, who teaches you what is best for you, who directs you in the way you should go.
ISAIAH 48:17 NIV

If ye keep watch over your hearts, and listen for the Voice of God and learn of Him, in one short hour ye can learn more from Him than ye could learn from man in a thousand years.
JOHANNES TAULER

Lord, I know You want me to read Your Word,
but sometimes I have a hard time doing so. With all
of my duties and responsibilities, it's easy to put off
Bible reading until later. But then "later" becomes days
and even weeks! Forgive me for neglecting the scriptures.
Help me to see that reading them is a privilege and a blessing,
not just another duty to cross off my list. Amen.

His Still, Small Voice

Draw nigh to God,
and he will draw nigh to you.
JAMES 4:8 KJV

We love to hear God's voice. His kind, affirming words lend boldness and confidence. No enemy is too fierce and no circumstance too great. But when we cease to hear from Him, we become fretful and troubled. Even His chastisement is preferred over silence, because reproof assures us that we are indeed His children. Our heart craves communion with the Lord. When it's lacking, we feel it to the depths of our soul.

Even when we cannot sense God's presence, faith assures us that He is near. But sometimes His distance is a result of our own carelessness. Our daily journeys to the throne of grace are sometimes postponed while we attend to louder demands. If those delays become habit, we may eventually find ourselves neglecting prayer altogether.

In order to hear God's still, small voice, we must draw as near to Him as possible. Prayer cannot be reserved for times of crisis and need. We must meet with our heavenly Father daily, even if we can't make it to our secret prayer closet. God isn't picky about time or place. He'll listen to us when we're up to our elbows in dishwater, in the rocking chair with a fussy baby, or driving down the highway.

Nothing is sweeter to the soul than hearing God's voice, and nothing thrills Him more than hearing from you. Have you been to His throne today?

Rejoicing in Jesus

Rejoice in the Lord always:
and again I say, Rejoice.
PHILIPPIANS 4:4 KJV

Joyful Christians are strong Christians. That's why our adversary works so hard to discourage us. Nothing takes the fight out of a child of God like a good dose of depression. And there's plenty in this world to be depressed about. But though we face tribulations in this life, Jesus told us to be of good cheer. He overcame the world, and through His grace and power, we can, too.

Joy doesn't come from what we own, or how we feel. All of those things are fleeting. But the joy of the Lord runs deep, springing from a divine well that can't be stopped up by earthly woes. It puts a smile on our face when we have reason to scowl. It picks us up when life lays us flat. It turns our complaints into praises and our tears into laughter. Even in times of deepest despair, we find the strength to keep calm and carry on.

Heaven-bound souls can't linger in the dumps for long, and if you find yourself there, it's time to take action. Boot out those joy robbers with praise. Put on some worship music and make a joyful noise unto the Lord. Sing a hymn, if only to yourself. Recount your blessings, naming each one to God in prayer. Most of all, keep your eyes on Jesus. The only way to overcome the world's sorrows is to stay focused on Him.

Be still, and know that I am God.
PSALM 46:10 KJV

When was the last time you laughed for the sheer joy of
your salvation? People are not attracted to somber doctrines.
There is no persuasive power in a gloomy and morbid religion.
Let the world see your joy, and you won't be able to keep
them away. To be filled with God is to be filled with joy.
UNKNOWN

Lord, my soul craves to spend time alone with You,
even though my flesh doesn't. There are so many things
to distract me from Your throne of grace. Some of them
aren't even important! Show me how to organize my schedule
so that I am using my time wisely instead of wasting it
on frivolous things. Help me to keep my priorities in order,
making sure that You stay in first place. Amen.

Gathering for Praise

*Enter into his gates with thanksgiving, and into his courts
with praise: be thankful unto him, and bless his name.*
PSALM 100:4 KJV

We can meet with the Lord anywhere and at any time, but
worshipping Him alone on a mountaintop doesn't encourage others
or enlighten ourselves. God wants all of His people to worship
together in unity and fellowship. It doesn't much matter where that
meeting takes place. As long as two or three are gathered in Jesus'
name, He's there, too (Matthew 18:20).

Church is a place of praise. God isn't glorified when we attend
services out of habit or duty, then sit in our pew like the proverbial
bump on a log. His Word tells us to teach and admonish one another
"in psalms and hymns and spiritual songs, singing with grace in your
hearts to the Lord" (Colossians 3:16 KJV).

Like everyone else, Christians get weary and discouraged. But
when we belong to God's great family, we never have to weep alone.
Church is a place to share our burdens, pray for them together, and
rejoice as one when the answer finally comes.

If you don't have a church home, you're missing out on
something special. Finding one can seem overwhelming, but when we
ask God to lead us to the right body of believers, He will be faithful
to do so. Take time for church this Sunday. You might be surprised
at what the Lord has in store there for you.

Cast Your Crown

But God forbid that I should glory,
save in the cross of our Lord Jesus Christ.
GALATIANS 6:14 KJV

The crown is a symbol of victory. Kings of old didn't get to wear them unless first there had been bloodshed. Ancient powers were always struggling to reign over each other, and when one finally conquered, he earned the right to wear the crown.

Jesus is our conqueror. He triumphed over the forces of evil, winning eternal life for every soul that comes to Him in repentance. And when His shed blood pours over our sinful heart, washing it clean, we receive that crown of life. It is the first of many victories won for us by our Savior, the first of many crowns.

When we are risen from the mire of our sinful past to walk in newness of life, old things are passed away. We begin to reap the blessings of home and family. Others may be influenced by our example and drawn to Christ. God may bestow us with talents and abilities, perhaps even a position of leadership at church.

As we glory in the abundance of our redeemed life, remember who deserves the crown. As soon as it is placed on our head, let us kneel before the Savior and cast it at His feet. Without Him we are nothing. Each victory won, each grace we exhibit, each and every blessing in life, is given to us through the blood of the Lamb.

He alone is worthy.

Glorious

Whatsoever ye do, do all to the glory of God.
1 CORINTHIANS 10:31 KJV

More beautiful than snow-peaked mountains and glowing sunsets, more amazing than the intricate workings of the human body, more wonderful than anything our minds can imagine is God's power to change lives. When broken marriages are healed and restored; when wounded hearts forgive and goodness repays evil; when the vilest sinner is transformed into a child of heaven, then is God truly glorified.

There are no words sufficient to describe salvation, but we know when it has taken place. Changed hearts are revealed by changed actions. The cursing tongue brings forth blessings. The lustful heart becomes chaste. Selfish souls put others first, and liars are freed to tell the truth.

God is glorified when His light shines through us, not only in times of calamity or great sorrow but also in simple everyday life. We don't have to preach the Gospel in distant lands or minister to the sick and dying in order to shine for Christ. We need only to obey the Word of the Lord. When we follow Christ's example in our home and community, we testify of the power of the cross. Because without it, we can't love our neighbor or endure injustice. We can't manifest the fruits of the spirit or remain steadfast in times of temptation. But we can do all these things and more through Christ, who strengthens us.

Such is the power of our great Redeemer, and it is glorious.

Let your light so shine before men, that they
may see your good works, and glorify
your Father which is in heaven.
MATTHEW 5:16 KJV

When God makes His presence felt through us,
we are like the burning bush: Moses never took
any heed what sort of bush it was—he only
saw the brightness of the Lord.
GEORGE ELIOT

Lord, I want to mirror the actions of Jesus in everything
I do. Sometimes it seems impossible, when I think of my
shortcomings and weaknesses. But I don't have to go in my
own strength. Your Word tells me that I can do all things
through Christ who makes me strong. Help me to claim
that promise so I can let Your glory shine in me. Amen.

Amazing Grace

Amazing grace! How sweet the sound
That saved a wretch like me.
I once was lost, but now am found,
Was blind, but now I see.

'Twas grace that taught my heart to fear,
And grace my fears relieved.
How precious did that grace appear
The hour I first believed.

Through many dangers, toils and snares
I have already come;
'Tis grace hath brought me safe thus far
And grace will lead me home.

When we've been there ten thousand years
Bright shining as the sun,
We've no less days to sing God's praise
Than when we've first begun.

JOHN NEWTON, 1779

Born in London in 1725, as a child John Newton learned about God from his devout mother, who dreamed of his one day becoming a preacher. But her untimely death when he was young left him in the care of his father, a wild sea captain. He joined his father at sea at age eleven, and eventually became the captain of a slave-trading ship. His heart far from God, he led a life of sin and debauchery.

But God wasn't done with him yet. During a violent storm at sea in 1748 he cried out to the Lord to spare his life. God heard his prayer, and from that moment grace began to work in John Newton's heart. Eventually he gave up seafaring and became a well-respected minister, impacting many lives, including William Wilberforce, the man who abolished the slave trade in England. Out of a full and grateful heart, Newton penned "Amazing Grace" in the 1760s.

Amazing Grace!
How Sweet the Sound

The grace of our Lord was poured out on me abundantly,
along with the faith and love that are in Christ Jesus.
1 TIMOTHY 1:14 NIV

The amazing grace of the Lord is beyond our understanding.
Think of it: Adam and Eve, made by a loving Creator, enjoyed pure
fellowship with Him in the Garden of Eden. But through an act of
their will, sin entered in. What was a relationship of trust and love
was ruined by the sinful nature of the very beings God created. Man
and woman's disobedience created a barrier between them and God—
but the story didn't end there. The Creator, from His heart of love,
provided a way to restore the relationship that had been lost. How?
Through His grace—unmerited favor! God sent His Son to die so
that believers could live forever with Him. He has given us what we
don't deserve so that we can remain with Him in all ways—and for
all our days! What a loving Savior! This grace is nothing less than
amazing. No logic can explain it. Nothing we could ever say or do
could make us worthy. But the God of the universe—the One we
sinned against—has put in place a plan that removes the curse of
death. His sacrifice gives us freedom. His pain brings us healing.
His death grants us life. That is unfathomable, amazing grace!

That Saved a Wretch Like Me

What a wretched man I am!
Who will rescue me from this body that is subject to death?
ROMANS 7:24 NIV

Wretch. The word itself sounds so unlovely—certainly not a term that
anyone would choose to describe himself. Focusing so much time and
attention on our outward appearance, in an attempt to have beautiful
skin, hair, and body, we balk at the thought that someone could
consider us despicable. Yet because of the deceitfulness of our hearts,
the term *wretched* describes us quite accurately. Our outer personae
is a glossy cover to a heart that may harbor pride, selfishness, envy,
hatred, unforgiveness—and more. Yet our maker can see beyond
our façade to the black marks of sin within. But because of His love,
Christ provided a way to save us from ourselves. Although wretched
in heart, humanity to Him was worthy of His sacrifice. Our sin
stains are washed away by the blood of Jesus, shed to cleanse the very
hearts that chose to wander from Him. How humbling that is! In His
compassion, He took on the unlovely heart and has found it lovely.

The Word became flesh and made his dwelling among us.
We have seen his glory, the glory of the one and only Son,
who came from the Father, full of grace and truth.
JOHN 1:14 NIV

We believe that the work of regeneration, conversion,
sanctification, and faith is not an act of man's free
will and power, but of the mighty, efficacious,
and irresistible grace of God.
CHARLES SPURGEON

Heavenly Father, thank You for Your grace. I realize I have
done nothing to earn it. In Your goodness, You have reached
out to me and saved me from my sin. Forgive me for the times
I take Your gift for granted and act as if I've done something to
deserve it. Help me to accept Your grace with a sincere heart,
yet without guilt, as You have promised me forgiveness when
I repent. Your grace is indeed amazing! Amen.

I Once Was Lost but Now Am Found

*"For the Son of Man came
to seek and to save the lost."*
LUKE 19:10 NIV

Getting lost is a lonely, frightening feeling. A child who wanders from his mother and cannot find his way back to her not only produces panic in himself, but in his mother as well. The two individuals who have long been a part of each other feel sorrow until they are reunited. Oh, the anguish the Father must have felt when His Son left Him to go to earth! Father and Son, who had been unified in heaven, were now separated. But God willed that Jesus come down to do an incredibly valuable act for humankind. Then the day finally came that the one Son would be sacrificed for all. The impact of taking on the sin of the world caused Jesus' Father to have to turn His back on His only Son. What grief!

But then what joy! Jesus conquered the sorrow. He was victorious over death and returned to heaven, reunited once again with the Father. And because of His selfless act we, who were once separated from God because of our sin, can now have a relationship with Him. There is no more fear or anguish. Praise the Lord that we who have sought God are no longer lost, but found!

Was Blind but Now I See

*"I have come as a light to shine in this dark world, so that all
who put their trust in me will no longer remain in the dark."*
JOHN 12:46 NLT

Have you ever tried to walk through your house in complete darkness?
Without even a glimmer of light, all you can see is blackness, regardless
of how much you squint. You know vaguely where pieces of furniture
and walls are, but you cannot distinguish them. You grope around to
feel any hidden dangers that may trip you up. The anxiety that you
could run into something, stub a toe, or fall flat on your face is very real.

That's a little like our spiritual life, before salvation. Prior to
accepting Christ, we try to make it through the darkness of sin
independently, steering around unseen dangers. But tragedy is certain
without a Savior. Without sight—and light—we cannot safely reach
the destination. But the moment we believe, God brings full sight to
our eyes that had previously failed. The path now becomes clear. Fear
subsides. Our days of wandering aimlessly are over. The destination
is evident. One look at the Savior's face brings comfort and strength.
And spiritual eyes are finally opened to see all the Father has in store
for believers.

And I am convinced that nothing can ever separate us from God's love. Neither death nor life, neither angels nor demons, neither our fears for today nor our worries about tomorrow—not even the powers of hell can separate us from God's love. No power in the sky above or in the earth below—indeed, nothing in all creation will ever be able to separate us from the love of God that is revealed in Christ Jesus our Lord.
ROMANS 8:38–39 NLT

Either sin is with you, lying on your shoulders, or it is lying on Christ, the Lamb of God. Now if it is lying on your back, you are lost; but if it is resting on Christ, you are free, and you will be saved. Now choose what you want.
MARTIN LUTHER

Jesus, oh the joy of being sought, then found! It is indeed a time of jubilation, a rejoicing that what was once separated is now restored and will never be alienated from You again. Thank You for pursuing me and finding me. I give to You my whole heart—my whole being—to use for Your glory. I want to be worthy of the joy You found in saving me from my sins. In Your name, amen.

The Hour I First Believed!

"For God so loved the world, that He gave His only begotten Son, that whoever believes in Him shall not perish, but have eternal life."
JOHN 3:16 NASB

Time dictates so much in life. There are clocks, electronic devices, and watches that constantly remind us of the hour. In our harried schedules, it's easy to be carried away by the clock. Chores, errands, and responsibilities are dictated by the ticking of old timepieces or pulsing of the new. And at day's end we attempt to recharge, with the hope of having enough stamina to make it through the routine the following day.

But in the Christian life, there is a definite shift in time—a moment when everything suddenly changes. The mundane ticking has faded away and things are different. It's the hour we first believe! The focus shifts from ourselves to God. Following the ways of the world has ended; pursuing a life with Jesus has begun. All of the old is gone; new life in Jesus is here! How simple it is over time, however, to return to that old, familiar ticking—our way of life before Jesus interceded. The feeling of newness can fade. The routine can become stagnant. Our Lord is patient and waits for us to reignite that fire. Today, decide to return to Him with the same passion you had the hour you first believed.

Through Many Dangers. . .
I Have Already Come

We can rejoice, too, when we run into problems and trials, for we know that
they help us develop endurance. And endurance develops strength of character,
and character strengthens our confident hope of salvation.
ROMANS 5:3–4 NLT

Adversity will affect each person's life at some point and can come
in different forms—financial troubles, health issues, and the loss of
loved ones. Unexpected trials can quickly sweep in, touching a life
with grief or anguish. Temptation can also come at any moment. If
given in to, confusion and consequences can follow in its wake. And
there are other countless, unforeseen dangers that have the potential
of changing the course of one's life.

But in all of these times of challenge, we can be assured that
nothing will reach God's child without His knowledge. He does not
cause the difficulty but is prepared to walk with His child through
it and provide strength when all human power is gone. What looks
like a hopeless situation to the world can be a season that brings the
believer even closer to her Lord. She, at the end of that challenging
season, can savor a sweet time of victory and glory to the One who
walked, or even carried, her through. Because we live in a world
touched by sin, sorrow will affect both unbeliever and believer alike.
But what a hope we who are in Christ have! We can draw close to the
Savior and rest in the comfort and peace that only He can give amid
the storm.

Seek the LORD while he may be found;
call on him while he is near.
ISAIAH 55:6 NIV

So often we have a kind of vague, wistful longing that
the promises of Jesus should be true. The only way
really to enter into them is to believe them with the
clutching intensity of a drowning man.
WILLIAM BARCLAY

Heavenly Father, thank You for the hour I first believed.
I am awed You loved me so much that You prepared a way
for me to come to You and enjoy a relationship with You.
Please help me not to become complacent in my spiritual walk.
May the joy of fellowship mark each moment of my days as I
cling to You and Your Word. May I wake tomorrow with
even more excitement at the thought of communing with You.
In Jesus' name, amen.

'Tis Grace Hath Brought Me Safe Thus Far

Let us then approach God's throne of grace with confidence, so that we may receive mercy and find grace to help us in our time of need.
HEBREWS 4:16 NIV

An adult will often prepare to cross a street with a cursory glance left and right for oncoming traffic before crossing. A child, however, needs help in getting from one side to the other. Although the child may think he can dodge traffic by himself, most kids—because of their size, limited experience, and not-yet-fully-developed peripheral vision—just don't have the ability to see all the dangers of oncoming traffic. With someone to hold his hand and lead, the child will reach the other side of the street safe and sound.

So it is with God. He can see the dangers around us, His children, and knows the best path for us to take. He offers His hand to lead us through potential unseen risks and guides us safely to our destination. Our Savior will gently lead you through troubles, but there are also times that His gracious hand will pick you up. The path may seem too long and tiring. Human strength can fail, and it is at those moments that God will lovingly carry you through the difficulty.

And Grace Will Lead Me Home

Being justified by his grace, we should be made heirs according to the hope of eternal life.
TITUS 3:7 KJV

You may travel for your job or for personal pleasure. Perhaps you have saved a lifetime for a special vacation to an exotic location. Or maybe it's a destination that has been slated to spend with family. Whether the goal of the trip is to secure a deal for the employer, enjoy magnificent scenery, or spend moments away from the hustle and bustle of life, there is one commonality that unites all travelers: the joy of returning home. No matter how much pleasure you may get in your time away, for most of us it's true that there's no place like home.

After this journey of life upon the earth, we, as God's children, will finally reach our destination—a home with Jesus Christ. He has been preparing for and awaiting our arrival. This heavenly home will be a place of perfection and joy, a place where Creator and created can relax together after the journey. What a blessing it will be to have the Savior look into our eyes and say, "Welcome home, child. I have been waiting for you."

In him we have redemption through his blood, the forgiveness of sins,
in accordance with the riches of God's grace that he lavished on us.
EPHESIANS 1:7–8 NIV

Saving faith is an immediate relation to Christ, accepting,
receiving, resting upon Him alone, for justification,
sanctification, and eternal life by virtue of God's grace.
CHARLES SPURGEON

Lord Jesus, thank You for the gracious way You care for me.
Your faithfulness and gentleness have brought me this far
along my life's path, and I am confident that You will not leave
me now. You partner with me, walking beside me all the way,
leading me in the paths I should go, and keeping me from harm.
I have full assurance that I can entrust my life to You and to
Your direction. In Your name, amen.

The Lord Has Promised Good to Me

Give thanks to the LORD, for he is good.
PSALM 136:1 NIV

God has promised good. He does not guarantee that only good things will happen, simply that everything that comes from Him will be worked out for good in the life of the believer. We will be parted from loved ones by death. A job that we've had for ten years may be lost. Illness or injury will touch our lives. From a human perspective, none of these things seem "good" and may bring overwhelming grief.

But God's ways are so different from ours. What we view as a tragedy, Christ can use as a catalyst to bring about His great work. If a loved one chooses salvation as a result of our trial, can we then see the goodness? If, after we've suffered a loss, a wayward son or daughter returns to the Savior, does that lessen the grief in a small way? Entrusting our life to the Lord is a daily act of discipline. He will shower blessings of goodness on His believers. And He will take hardships and use them for His good—and ours, although we may not see it until years down the road, if at all. He has promised goodness. And we, as His followers, must choose to fully trust Him, for He always keeps His promises.

His Word My Hope Secures

*Then He opened their minds
to understand the Scriptures.*
LUKE 24:45 NASB

Instruction manuals come with most new electronics and appliances. Some note the best operating conditions. Others detail the specifications of the unit and the parts. Still others offer information on how to get assistance if the device malfunctions or a repair or replacement is needed. Unfortunately, most of us are guilty of tossing the manual aside, saving it only for when difficulty arises or troubleshooting is required.

God's Word should not be treated like an expendable instruction manual, consulted only when problems come or the occasional question arises. For the Bible is the instruction book that God gave us for life. His intention is that we read, study, and memorize it. The more we are familiar with what's inside it, the better we can know our God and His will for our lives. God's Word is exciting. It is powerful. It offers comfort to His followers. It provides instruction for our Christian walk. Our loving Father has not left us on our own to figure things out. He has given us His Word to study, cherish, and follow daily.

O taste and see that the LORD is good:
blessed is the man that trusteth in him.
PSALM 34:8 KJV

It is not the will of God to give us more troubles than
will bring us to live by faith on him; he loves us too well
to give us a moment of uneasiness but for our good.
WILLIAM ROMAINE

Jesus, Your Word reveals that You have good things in
store for me. In Your goodness, You saved me by Your
grace. You love me with unconditional, everlasting love.
You are slow to get angry with me. You meet my physical,
emotional, mental, and spiritual needs. Your ways are so
much higher than mine. Because of all this I continue
to trust that You will keep me in Your care today and
forevermore. In Your name, amen.

He Will My Shield and Portion Be

My flesh and my heart may fail,
but God is the strength of my heart
and my portion forever.
PSALM 73:26 NIV

God is the shield and portion for His followers—He is the defense and all-sufficient provision of those who believe in Him. The use of a shield implies that for Christians, there will be times of attack. However, God hasn't said, "I will give you a shield." He has declared, "I will *be* your shield." He wants us to run to Him, to hide behind Him as the battle intensifies. Imagine children playing a game of tag. If there is an adult nearby, the kid being chased might try to hide behind the adult, creating a barrier between himself and his chaser. That's what Christ wants to be—the barrier between His beloved and the one attempting to bring harm.

In Psalm 73:25, the psalmist asks, "Whom have I in heaven but you? And earth has nothing I desire besides you" (NIV). Thus God, our portion, is also our all-satisfying inheritance. He is the only thing that can truly make our souls sing with joy, now and forever!

When it feels as if you're in the line of fire, run to your Savior. He is a willing shield, ready to deflect any harm. And He is all we need. There is no end to Him, His love, or His goodness.

A Life of Joy and Peace

May the God of hope fill you with all joy and peace as you trust in him,
so that you may overflow with hope by the power of the Holy Spirit.
ROMANS 15:13 NIV

What a pleasant thought! A life of *joy* and *peace*, words that typically appear in carols at Christmastime. Yet God desires that His children live lives characterized by joy and peace throughout the year. The word *joy* is often equated with an outward sign of happiness. Although joy can be exhibited that way, it is more of a heart matter—one that may not necessarily be evidenced by a smile, but by a spirit of contentment, not to be based on happenings or circumstances but on the depth of our relationship with our Savior, the source of true joy.

Peace can be obtained and retained in moments of quiet solitude, and even in the midst of turmoil. For that peace is a state of restfulness, a quieting of the spirit. Christ Himself demonstrated the need to spend quiet time independently. He most often did so to talk with His Father. In the same way, we should imitate Christ's actions and set some quiet time aside to commune with Him. The more times we do, the more we will experience a life of joy and peace—before, during, and after the storm.

The LORD is good,
A stronghold in the day of trouble;
And He knows those who trust in Him.
NAHUM 1:7 NKJV

Spread out your petition before God, and then say,
"Thy will, not mine, be done." The sweetest lesson I have
learned in God's school is to let the Lord choose for me.
D. L. MOODY

Heavenly Father, thank You for being my shield of
protection. I trust in You—I never have to fear that
anything will happen to me that will catch You off guard.
You protect me from both seen and unseen dangers.
You are watchful on all sides and at all times. Satan's fiery
darts cannot penetrate Your defenses. Thank You for
being my safe place where I can hide to escape the dangers
that threaten me. In Jesus' name, amen.

But God. . .
Will Be Forever Mine

There is a friend who sticks closer than a brother.
PROVERBS 18:24 NIV

God's Word tells us He always has been, is, and always will be. He has no beginning, and He will have no end. Our minds cannot comprehend that, but it is comforting to rest in His steadfastness. Yet as amazing as His *foreverness* is, His promises go even further. He not only is a God who is not bound by time, but He longs to have a relationship for all eternity with the people He created. It now becomes personal.

Just as God is pursuing His children, He wants us to pursue a relationship with Him. He eagerly desires our hearts to be fully His as we journey through life, seeking after Him. But the benefit of a relationship with Him doesn't end there. When the day comes for us to cross the line from the finite to the infinite, the connection continues. And we will then be present with the Savior in heaven forever! God has promised you, His child, that when you call on Him, He will save you, and you will be forever His. Out of a heart of love for Him, you can happily declare that God is sticking with you from now until the end of time. He has been, is, and always will be "forever yours."

When We've Been There Ten Thousand Years

A day is like a thousand years to the LORD,
and a thousand years is like a day.
2 PETER 3:8 NLT

Ten thousand years! Considering that from a human perspective, it seems like a long time. But God's system is a different one—so contrary to what we experience. He does not have to glance at a wristwatch or take a peek at a cell phone to stay on schedule. The seconds and minutes do not get away from Him. How liberating it would be to go on a vacation and not be constrained by time. To remove your watch and simply enjoy the day certainly promotes relaxation. Most of us would want to stay and enjoy the freedom of this kind of lifestyle as long as possible. But eventually there is a return to schedules and deadlines. Once again, we're forced to consult our dials and digital displays.

In heaven, there will never be any more darkness. No more clocks. All of the days dictated by a timepiece will be a thing of the past. Time will cease to exist. We will simply be with our Savior. We will reunite with loved ones and meet other believers. There will be singing—true worship. There will be feasting. And there will be joy. . .joy like we have never known before.

We've No Less Days. . . Than When We'd First Begun

Praise the LORD.
Praise God in his sanctuary;
praise him in his mighty heavens.
PSALM 150:1 NIV

God created us to worship Him and have a relationship with Him. He longs to hear our words and songs of praise. He alone deserves our endless adoration. He is the glorious God who will never leave us, the gracious Savior who has prepared a special place for us, and the Holy Spirit who will forever guide us.

When a believer leaves this world and enters heaven, he will begin his song of praise to our three-in-one God. The new song will begin and have no end. This act of adoration will not be a task-oriented performance; it will flow from a heart full of love for God.

Here on earth, the believer's communication with the Lord is through prayer—the conduit through which we worship Him, make requests of Him, confess our faults to Him, and thank Him. But on entry into heaven, there will be a new way to communicate. We will be in His presence and able to speak directly to Him! There will be no more requests or confessions—simply worship and thanksgiving.

Our desire to worship the God who showered us with grace will be a natural one. We will put our love for Him into word and song—true praise of the One who saved us and loves us with an everlasting love.

Listen, I tell you a mystery: We will not all sleep, but we will all be changed—in a flash, in the twinkling of an eye, at the last trumpet. For the trumpet will sound, the dead will be raised imperishable, and we will be changed. For the perishable must clothe itself with the imperishable, and the mortal with immortality. When the perishable has been clothed with the imperishable, and the mortal with immortality, then the saying that is written will come true: "Death has been swallowed up in victory."
1 CORINTHIANS 15:51–54 NIV

The best moment of a Christian's life is his last one, because it is the one that is nearest heaven. And then it is that he begins to strike the keynote of the song which he shall sing to all eternity.
CHARLES SPURGEON

Father, my mind is limited by earthly time, so it is difficult for me to even begin to imagine eternity. My waking is ruled by the clock, as are events and meals throughout the day. And time dictates what time I go to bed. But in heaven, there will be no need for sleeping or eating. There will be no obligations. There will be no darkness. I long for the joy of spending eternity with You! In Jesus' name, amen.

It Is Well with My Soul

When peace, like a river, attendeth my way,
When sorrows like sea billows roll;
Whatever my lot, Thou has taught me to say,
It is well, it is well, with my soul.

Refrain
It is well, with my soul,
It is well, with my soul,
It is well, it is well, with my soul.

Though Satan should buffet, though trials should come,
Let this blest assurance control,
That Christ has regarded my helpless estate,
And hath shed His own blood for my soul.

My sin—oh, the bliss of this glorious thought—
My sin—not in part but the whole,
Is nailed to the cross, and I bear it no more,
Praise the Lord, praise the Lord, O my soul!

And Lord, haste the day when my faith shall be sight,
The clouds be rolled back as a scroll;
The trump shall resound, and the Lord shall descend,
Even so—it is well with my soul.

Horatio G. Spafford, 1873

Life was good for Horatio Spafford in the late 1860s. A successful Christian lawyer, he and his wife lived in a posh suburb of Chicago with their five children. Then tragedy struck in 1870 when their four-year-old son died of scarlet fever. A year later the Great Chicago Fire wiped out most of his real estate holdings in the city and brought them close to financial ruin. Yet the Spaffords didn't despair. They used what little resources they had to reach out to others in greater need.

But their troubles weren't over. In 1873 Spafford's wife and daughters were on their way to Europe when their ship was struck by another ocean liner and all four of their daughters were drowned. Spafford wasted no time boarding a ship to join his heartbroken wife in England. When his ship passed over the site of the crash, he was inspired to write the words of the beloved hymn "It Is Well with My Soul," a song that has touched countless lives.

Peace Like a River

*"I will extend peace to her like a river,
and the wealth of nations like a flooding stream."*
ISAIAH 66:12 NIV

The Romans defined peace—*pax*—as *"absentia belli,"* the absence of war. Today we might use *peace* as meaning an absence of disturbance or noise. So what inspired Isaiah and, centuries later, the hymn writer Horatio G. Spafford, to compare peace to a river? Jesus described the new life He offered as "rivers of living water" that flowed from the inside out (John 7:38). The water of life flows like a river through heaven (Revelation 22:1).

Even small creeks and rivers must move. If they don't, they become stagnant and unable to support life. Grandfathers might take their grandchildren fishing to a quiet spot by a gently flowing stream. A few miles downstream that same river explodes into rapids as it pushes its way past rocks and beyond that, plunges into a waterfall. A river represents movement—not an absence of disturbance. The truth is that turbulence brings life, even abundant life. Salmon fight their way upstream to spawn. Water surges over dams to provide electricity. Instead of wishing for peace like that unmoving, stagnant pond, pray for the flowing river of God's living water that will bring life and peace.

Sorrows Like Sea Billows

I cried by reason of mine affliction unto the LORD,
and he heard me. . . . For thou hadst cast me into the deep, in the
midst of the seas. . .all thy billows and thy waves passed over me.
JONAH 2:2—3 KJV

Losing a loved one is one of the most painful experiences anyone can experience. Losing a child is uniquely excruciating. But losing every last one of your children produces crushing grief almost beyond endurance. Horatio Spafford experienced that depth of pain when he lost first one child to sickness and then his four daughters in a tragic accident at sea. His wife, whose life was spared, brokenly told her husband when he rejoined her that her girls had been ripped from her arms by the turbulent waters. Knowing this history adds poignancy to his choice of words in the first verse: "When sorrows like sea billows roll."

The longer we live, the more aware we become of the sorrows life's storms send rolling our way. Often, like Spafford, our sorrows involve losing family—parents, spouses, children—through disagreements, illness, even death. Like Jonah in the verses above, we can cry out to the Lord in our affliction and know that He hears us. If He casts us into the deep, He will also draw us out. Like Spafford, we can say in the midst of sorrow, "It is well with my soul."

*"Peace I leave with you; my peace I give you. I do not
give to you as the world gives. Do not let your
hearts be troubled and do not be afraid."*
JOHN 14:27 NIV

Sorrow comes in great waves. . .but rolls over us, and though
it may almost smother us, it leaves us. And we know that if it is
strong, we are stronger, inasmuch as it passes and we remain.
HENRY JAMES

Everlasting Father, thank You for Your Son, the Prince
of Peace. I thank You for the promise of that peace to me.
Forgive me when I allow the anxiety in my heart to overpower
Your peace. Make the peace that is like a river flow in and
through me, that I may experience Your peace and share it with
others. May I grow in that peace by obedience to Your will
and Your desires for my life. Amen.

Whatever My Lot

*I know that my redeemer lives, and that in the end he will
stand on the earth. And after my skin has been destroyed, yet in
my flesh I will see God; I myself will see him with my own eyes—
I, and not another. How my heart yearns within me!*
JOB 19:25–27 NIV

The earliest written of biblical accounts, the book of Job addresses the age-old question: Why do bad things happen to good people? Job had family, fortune, and health. After Satan received permission from God, all was stripped away. Instead of complaining, Job said, "Blessed be the name of the Lord." In the end, God restored Job's earlier status.

When Job was in the middle, stuck between loss and restoration, his friends exhorted him to confess his sins. In defense of his innocence, he made a remarkable declaration of faith. "My redeemer lives! And He is my judge." In good times and bad, when Job had friends aplenty as well as when everyone turned against him, he kept his eyes on the living God. The prospect of bringing his case before God excited him. You may not experience a complete reversal of fortune like Job, but some days will seem better than others. Whatever your lot, make your daily prayer, "Blessed be the name of the Lord. I will see God—nothing can be more exciting!"

Trials Should Come

"I told you these things so that you can have peace in me. In this world you will have troubles, but be brave! I have defeated the world."
JOHN 16:33 NCV

A woman came to God with a complaint. "God, I feel like You've given me the biggest cross. Please let me exchange it for a smaller one." With a gentle smile, God took the woman to a closed door. "In this room, you will find everyone's cross. You can choose the one you prefer to carry." Walking into the room, the woman dropped her burden on the ground. Some crosses reached to the ceiling. She rushed past those. On other, smaller ones, the wood was heavier. She didn't want those either. As she examined the crosses, she rejected one after another. At last she found a small, insignificant cross, hidden under the weight of the others. Convinced she had made the best choice, she left the room. When God saw her leave, He said, "That's the cross you carried in."

Trials will come. Jesus said so. The Bible talks about trials as if they are gifts from a loving Father. They produce joy, hope, and perseverance and prove genuine faith. But like the woman in the story, most people want to exchange their troubles for an easier load. Every person has trials, or tests, fitted to her needs. Count your cross as a joy. Remember it is made for you.

We know that God is always at work for the good of everyone who loves him. They are the ones God has chosen for his purpose.
ROMANS 8:28 CEV

Trials teach us what we are; they dig up the soil,
and let us see what we are made of; they just
turn up some of the ill weeds onto the surface.
CHARLES SPURGEON

Almighty God, I rest in Your sovereign care. Everything
that happens to me, good or bad, You work in Your
purpose for my life. Forgive me for complaining about
what You have given me for today. Teach me to trust
You in all that I do. Keep my eyes focused on the
Giver and not on the gifts given. Amen.

Blessed Assurance

*Paul, a servant of God and an apostle of Jesus Christ to further
the faith of God's elect and their knowledge of the truth that
leads to godliness — in the hope of eternal life, which God,
who does not lie, promised before the beginning of time.*
TITUS 1:1–2 NIV

Life insurance, health insurance, warranty, guarantee: TV commercials
and Internet ads shout these words at us, but how reliable are these
promises? Politicians are particularly guilty of often promising
something they cannot deliver. In 1988, presidential candidate
George H. W. Bush famously promised, "Read my lips: no new
taxes." His opponents delighted when he agreed to an increase in
taxes two years later.

Fifty-one years before Bush, British Prime Minister Neville
Chamberlain reached an agreement guaranteeing peace with Hitler.
He told his countrymen, "I believe it is peace for our time. . . peace
with honor." Within two years, Britain was pulled into the war. The
world craves certainty yet finds it an elusive quality. Promises given
in good faith often cannot be kept. Four centuries ago French author
Francois de la Rochefoucauld said, "The only thing constant in life
is change." Blessed assurance! One thing in life has not changed and
never will: God is the same yesterday, today, and tomorrow. What He
promises, He can and will perform. The Christian's hope is based on
the unchanging God.

My Helpless Estate

They came into this world naked, and when they die,
they will be just as naked. They can't take anything with them,
and they won't have anything to show for all their work.
ECCLESIASTES 5:15 CEV

To get a glimpse of our helplessness as human beings, there are just two places you need to visit: a hospital's maternity unit and a nursing home. A newborn baby relies on doctors, nurses, and then Mom and Dad to take care of her every need. Unable to feed, clothe, clean, or care for herself, there are dozens of basic necessities that she is helpless to do for herself—both physically and developmentally. At the other end of life, she may need the assistance of nursing care when she needs help with the basics of personal care. The causes range from a debilitating illness such as multiple sclerosis or Alzheimer's disease, to accidents, to the physical ravages of old age.

Helpless when we're born into the world, we humans often again become helpless as death approaches. Solomon understood this truth well. At birth, he was naked and poor. At death, the same would be true. In between, whatever wealth or power he acquired—or lost— came from God. The truth is, that no matter what helpless state you might be facing, God is still in control. He watches over us and protects us, especially when we are most vulnerable. The Lord cares deeply about our helpless estate—old, young, and in-between—and through it all, He acts on our behalf.

Blessed be the God and Father of our Lord Jesus Christ! According to his great mercy, he has caused us to be born again to a living hope through the resurrection of Jesus Christ from the dead.
1 PETER 1:3 ESV

Light for every darkness, life in death, the promise of
our Lord's return, and the assurance of everlasting glory.
D. L. MOODY

My God and Father, any hope I have in this life comes
from You. Your Son took my pain, my sin, my weakness
as His own. You have given me a guarantee for eternal life,
not on paper or because of premiums I have paid, but through
the blood of Your Son and by Your Holy Spirit. Forgive me
when I doubt and my faith falters. Use me for Your glory.

Shed His Own Blood

And almost all things are by the law purged with blood;
and without shedding of blood is no remission.
HEBREWS 9:22 KJV

How do you feel about blood? Does the sight of it (or maybe just the thought of it) make you queasy? Our twenty-first-century society has a fascination with blood. Pop culture has romanticized the vampire legend through books, movies, and TV shows. But humankind's interest in blood isn't really a new phenomenon. It extends far back in time. Many world religions throughout history demand a blood sacrifice. The ancient Aztecs even believed a human heart torn from a living body was the only thing that kept the sun rising every day.

In the twentieth century, doctors began the widespread practice of giving blood transfusions to patients who had lost a great deal of blood in accidents, disease, and during surgery. Without this infusion of new blood, death was inevitable. Blood is associated with both life and death. How fitting, then, that the blood Jesus willingly gave on the cross meant both His death and our life. The power of His blemish-free, sinless blood holds the key to His resurrection and our everlasting life with Him in heaven. Hallelujah!

My Sin Is Nailed to the Cross

Who will bring any charge against those whom God has chosen?
It is God who justifies. Who then is the one who condemns?
No one. Christ Jesus who died—more than that, who was raised
to life—is at the right hand of God and is also interceding for us.
ROMANS 8:33–34 NIV

A mother hears the sound of glass breaking. She runs into the living room to learn what has happened. Her favorite lamp, a delicate porcelain base holding the light bulb and shade, is shattered, scattered across the floor. Two guilty figures surround the mess: her six-year-old and her two-year-old. The boys look at each other, and in unison they point to each other. "He did it."

In that instant, the mother wishes she had a video camera to replay the last few minutes in the living room. But all she can do is question her children and decide who is lying and who is telling the truth. Like Lady Justice, the mother seeks to administer justice blindly, without favoritism. God doesn't need blinders. He sees the scales of justice clearly. The only weight equal to sin is death; and Jesus' death equals the weight of all sin for all time. In God's courtroom, He is judge, prosecutor, and defense counsel. Your sin. His cross. He paid the price—for you.

*He gives strength to the weary
and increases the power of the weak.*
ISAIAH 40:29 NIV

There is a sacredness in tears. They are not the mark of
weakness, but of power. They speak more eloquently
than ten thousand tongues. They are messengers of
overwhelming grief. . .and unspeakable love.
WASHINGTON IRVING

Holy God, how dare I come before You? I am born sinful,
weak, helpless, and foolish. How I thank You for offering
Your own Son to destroy sin and its power over me. On my
own, I cannot overcome sin. You offer compassion and mercy
for my helpless estate. Forgive my sin, O Lord. Make me
obedient to Your Holy Spirit as He transforms me
into Your holy image.

I Bear It No More

"Come to me, all you who are weary and burdened,
and I will give you rest. Take my yoke upon you and learn
from me, for I am gentle and humble in heart, and you will find
rest for your souls. For my yoke is easy and my burden is light."
MATTHEW 11:28–30 NIV

Does your exercise routine include lifting weights? Maybe you tone a little bit with a dumbbell or two, or maybe you spend a few minutes after cardio on a weight machine. Some female Olympic weightlifters have lifted more than four hundred pounds in their events. Talk about a heavy burden. Not many women are weightlifters, but we all know what it means to carry a heavy load. It may mean a literal load such as a child on our back and grocery bags in each hand. It may be a burdened schedule, juggling family, work, and ministry. It may be emotional baggage from the past. Everyone carries the load of sin and earns its paycheck, death.

What are you burdened with today? Most of us would welcome someone to share the yoke, to help carry the load. In Jesus, we find the perfect weightlifting partner—because He takes it all. He gives rest to the weary. He won't reprimand us for being too weak. He removes our heavy weight of sin and returns a light burden in its place. Go to Him—or better yet, ask Him to come to you if you can't carry your burden any farther—and find rest for your soul.

Hence to Live

I appeal to you therefore, brothers, by the mercies of God,
to present your bodies as a living sacrifice, holy and
acceptable to God, which is your spiritual worship.
ROMANS 12:1 ESV

In the Old Testament, when a priest made a sacrifice of a blemish-free animal, it meant that animal's death. So for Paul to encourage the church in Rome to offer their lives as a living sacrifice to God, the term may have seemed like an oxymoron. The truth is, because of what Jesus did on the cross, He has every right to require a sacrifice from us. But if we gave up everything—even our very lives—it wouldn't fulfill the debt we owe Him.

Instead, we can live as living sacrifices by dedicating our lives—our years here on earth—to give glory to Him. That could mean something life-changing like going into full-time mission work, sharing the good news to the ends of the earth. But maybe today that means sharing with someone in need in the name of Jesus. Or it might mean taking an extra moment to chat with a coworker who is having a rough day and then praying for her. Considering what Jesus has done, offering yourself as a living sacrifice is only right and natural. Today, live like Christ, for Christ, by faith in Christ, and you'll find an abundant life in Him.

According to the foreknowledge of God the Father, in the sanctification of the Spirit, for obedience to Jesus Christ and for sprinkling with his blood: May grace and peace be multiplied to you.
1 PETER 1:2 ESV

This is faith: a renouncing of everything we are apt
to call our own and relying wholly upon the blood,
righteousness, and intercession of Jesus.
JOHN NEWTON

God, how I thank You that I am adopted into Your family
by the blood of Your Son. You chose me as Your child before
the foundation of the world. Forgive me for the times I am a
disobedient daughter, when I live to please myself and not You.
Day by day, minute by minute, teach me to remain in
You and to serve You in all I do.

In Death as in Life

O death, where is thy sting? O grave, where is thy victory?
The sting of death is sin; and the strength of sin is the law. But thanks
be to God, which giveth us the victory through our Lord Jesus Christ.
1 CORINTHIANS 15:55—57 KJV

Death finds everyone. It claims the elderly, at the end of a full life.
It claims the youngest ones who die before they are even born. It
claims people at every age in between. Like a young woman—just
twenty-four years old—who passed away suddenly. People filled the
sanctuary for her memorial service, shocked at the loss of the sweet-
spirited girl. The house of worship was transformed into an assembly
of mourners.

The pastor shared the girl's testimony in her own words. Her
poetic expression of faith lifted grief into the realm of rejoicing.
"I look into Your face / a face of love and wonder / I shall find a
place called home in Your arms." No one listening could doubt that
she had gone on to her heavenly home. This death was not a final
good-bye, but only a temporary separation. As Paul admonished
the Thessalonians, the mourners rejoiced as those with hope. They
celebrated the victory given to the Christian through the Lord Jesus
Christ. Sooner or later, unless we are still living when Jesus returns, all
Christians will experience death. But because of His sacrifice on the
cross, death has lost its sting. The grave no longer has the final word
in the story of our lives. Thanks be to God!

The Sky Is Our Goal

*If you would tear open the skies
and come down to earth, then everything would change. . . .
No one has ever seen any God except you,
who does such great things for those who trust him.*
ISAIAH 64:1, 4 ERV

It's humanity's universal cry: "God, if only You would act. . ." Mary
and Martha appealed to their good friend, the miracle-worker Jesus,
to come when their brother lay dying. They *knew* what Jesus could do.
But Jesus didn't come, and Martha could only say, "Lord, if you had
been here, my brother would not have died" (John 11:21 ERV). Like
Isaiah, who also knew what God could do, Martha couldn't see any
reason for Jesus' silence. Today's reader knows the rest of the story,
that Jesus raised Lazarus from the dead, and the glory was given to
God. But for Mary and Martha, the days they spent waiting seemed
cruelly long.

That's where Christians live in this world—between the agony
of Good Friday and the final answer of the Resurrection—between
the new life received at salvation and the future new heaven and new
earth, when all things will be made new. So we wait for the return of
her Savior. Living by faith, we anticipate the end of the story. But we
know the final score. Death is only the portal to eternity—eternity
with our heavenly Father. Live today in the hope of the day when
God will tear open the skies and every eye on earth shall see Him.

[He] destroyed death and has brought life
and immortality to light through the good news.
2 TIMOTHY 1:10 NIV

I'll love Thee in life, I will love Thee in death,
And praise Thee as long as Thou givest me breath;
And say when the death dew lies cold on my brow,
If ever I loved Thee, My Jesus, 'tis now.
WILLIAM R. FEATHERSTONE

Peace-giving God, I have seen the peace that presides
at the death of loved ones who know You. When I walk
through that valley, whether in the shadows of someone
else's passing or as I take my final journey, You will give me
the same peace. Forgive me when I fear death, as those who
have no hope. Glorify Yourself in me, both in life and in death.

The Voice of the Lord

Behold, I stand at the door, and knock: if any man hear my voice, and open the door, I will come in to him, and will sup with him, and he with me.
REVELATION 3:20 KJV

Picture the sight: a mother holds her newborn baby, crooning in a quiet voice, "I love Jordan." The baby girl learns her identity through that soft voice. When that infant has grown into an active toddler, she scribbles on the walls. The first time, her mother corrects her gently. "Jordan, use crayons on paper, not on the walls." Jordan continues coloring. Her mother's voice grows more urgent. "Jordan Elizabeth, I told you to stop coloring on the walls." Ignoring the correction, Jordan continues. Speaking even more forcefully, the mother says, "JORDAN ELIZABETH FRANKLIN, go to time out NOW."

The Christian's relationship with God the Father works a lot like that. He longs to speak to us in the still, small voice that Elijah heard in the cave (1 Kings 19:12). He wants His children to open the door and invite Him in for a time of fellowship (Revelation 3:20). However, if believers don't listen, God can always get louder. He will do whatever is necessary to get their attention. And in the last day, God will come with a shout. Every eye will see Him and every ear will hear. Those who have never paid attention to His voice before will fall on their knees, terrified. Second Peter 3:9 (NIV) says, "The Lord is not slow in keeping his promise, as some understand slowness. Instead he is patient with you, not wanting anyone to perish, but everyone to come to repentance." Listen to God's still, small voice—before it becomes a shout.

My Faith Shall Be Sight

The city does not need the sun or the moon to shine on it,
for the glory of God gives it light, and the Lamb is its lamp.
REVELATION 21:23 NIV

The Last Battle, the final volume in the classic Chronicles of Narnia by C. S. Lewis, tells the end of the old Narnia. Everyone is sent to their proper place, except for a group of dwarves. They remain in the stable, where they only see darkness. Lucy begs Aslan to help them. In sorrow, the great Lion replies, "They will not let us help them. They have chosen cunning instead of belief. . .so afraid of being taken in that they cannot be taken out." They have chosen to shut their eyes to the light of Aslan's country.

Put yourself in the dwarves' place. They are only inches away from glory—but they have blinded themselves to it—too afraid to be taken advantage of. God's glory shines in the earth today. He can be seen in the face of a newborn baby, in the splendor of a sunset—in the fellowship of believers gathered in His name. Open your eyes to God's glory on this earth. Resist the temptation of becoming cynical and jaded toward His many miracles. Being aware of His presence, His holiness, His glory, will prepare your heart for an eternity in His full greatness.

It Is Well with My Soul

Praise the LORD, my soul; all my inmost being, praise his holy name.
Praise the LORD, my soul, and forget not all his benefits.
PSALM 103:1–2 NIV

In Psalm 103, David gave at least one reason per verse why the believer should praise God with all her soul. Perhaps hymn writer H. G. Spafford thought of David's words when he wrote the hymn, "It Is Well with My Soul." Consider the words of the song with Psalm 103 in mind:

- It is well with my soul because God "satisfies [my] desires with good things" (verse 5).
- My soul is in good standing with God because "[He] redeems [my] life from the pit and crowns [me] with love and compassion" (verse 4).
- I know what is right and good, because God's righteousness is made available to those "who keep His covenant and remember to obey His precepts" (verse 18).
- I am living well, because God "forgives all [my] sins and heals all [my] diseases" (verse 3).

In spite of everything Spafford endured in the loss of his children and his fortune, when he considered everything God had done in the past and would do in the future, he repeated, "It is well with my soul." When you are feeling far from "well," take a look at Spafford's hymn and David's psalm. You will come away with the assurance that with the help of the Holy Spirit, it can be well with your soul.

*Be merciful unto me, O God, be merciful unto me: for my
soul trusteth in thee: yea, in the shadow of thy wings will
I make my refuge, until these calamities be overpast.*
PSALM 57:1 KJV

Be still, my soul: when change and tears are past,
All safe and blessed we shall meet at last.
KATHARINA A. VON SCHLEGEL

In You, Father, my soul finds rest, only in You. Because my
hope is anchored in You, it reaches behind the curtain that
used to separate us. Forgive me when I allow worries, physical
distress, or circumstances to cloud that assurance. Encourage
me with the miracle of my creation, Your attention to each
detail of my being. Make me still before You;
let Your praise fill my mouth.

All Things Bright and Beautiful

Refrain:
All things bright and beautiful,
All creatures great and small,
All things wise and wonderful:
The Lord God made them all.

Each little flower that opens,
Each little bird that sings,
He made their glowing colors,
He made their tiny wings.

The purple headed mountains,
The river running by,
The sunset and the morning
That brightens up the sky.

The cold wind in the winter,
The pleasant summer sun,
The ripe fruits in the garden,
He made them every one.

He gave us eyes to see them,
And lips that we might tell
How great is God Almighty,
Who has made all things well.
MRS. CECIL F. ALEXANDER, 1848

In the mid-1800s, Mrs. Cecil Frances Alexander, wife of the Anglican bishop of Ireland, undertook to teach a group of children the meaning of the Apostles' Creed. Finding traditional teaching methods ineffective, she put her writing skills to work and penned a series of hymns based on various phrases of the creed. "All Creatures Great and Small" was based on the phrase "I believe in God, the Father Almighty, maker of heaven and earth," and each verse celebrates the beauty of all that God has created.

In 1848 she published the hymn in a volume called *Hymns for Little Children*, which was very popular during her lifetime. A generous woman, she donated the proceeds of the sales of her hymnbook to a school for the deaf.

Creator and Artist God

Then God said, "Let us make mankind in our image,
in our likeness, so that they may rule over the fish in the sea
and the birds in the sky, over the livestock and all the wild animals,
and over all the creatures that move along the ground."
GENESIS 1:26 NIV

You could have heard a pin drop in the museum foyer that day. A famous artist had agreed to paint there, on opening day. What had been a blank canvas was covered now with reds and pinks. His brushstrokes careful, the artist worked the colors together, shading just the right amount in just the right places.

Before leaving the museum that day, he declared the painting dedicated to the city, to art lovers young and old. He snatched up a narrow tipped brush and added his signature. An original!

We serve an artist God, you know? He looked upon a blank canvas waiting to be filled. He took up His pallet of blues and greens, zebra stripes, and blinding light. He spoke into existence a world of sights and sounds more perfect than any other artist ever dreamed of painting. He brought to life tall giraffes, screeching monkeys, and furry puppies. He crafted collages of pastels around the sun to start and close each day. But. . .when He had created all of this, the world was not finished. On the sixth day, God made man. You are the signature of Creator God. Made in His image, you bear His name.

The Heavens Declare the Glory of the Lord

The heavens declare the glory of God;
the skies proclaim the work of his hands.
PSALM 19:1 NIV

Jenn had prepared for this night for months. Her voice coach suggested resting on the day of the performance, but she had sneaked in a rehearsal that afternoon. She wanted the song to be perfect.

The church was packed. Jenn's song was beautiful. The praise band didn't miss a beat, and the lighting added so much to the presentation. While Jenn knew that the praise should go to God, she couldn't help feeling a bit of pride as the congregation stood and clapped when she had finished that last high note.

Driving home that night down a country road, Jenn noticed the stars shining brightly against the backdrop of the black sky. At the sight of the vast array of twinkling lights, Jenn wept. Away from the crowded church, in the stillness of God's creation, she realized that her song had been for her own glory. The next time Jenn sang in church, her heart had changed. She didn't worry about her appearance or the perfection of the notes. She used her musical gifts to bring glory to the Father—just as the stars in the night sky do.

The heavens declare the glory of the Lord. Likewise, may we.

Let the rivers clap their hands,
let the mountains sing together for joy.
PSALM 98:8 NIV

God writes the gospel not in the Bible alone,
but on trees and flowers and clouds and stars.
MARTIN LUTHER

Heavenly Father, so many times I walk right past the trees.
I don't notice the fluffy white clouds or appreciate the rain
that nurtures our earth. Your creation is full of beauty and
wonder. I thank You for this wonderful world that You have
made. May I be more mindful of Your creation today. Amen.

A Peace That Passes Understanding

Be anxious for nothing, but in everything by prayer and supplication,
with thanksgiving, let your requests be made known to God;
and the peace of God, which surpasses all understanding,
will guard your hearts and minds through Christ Jesus.
PHILIPPIANS 4:6—7 NKJV

Have you ever been tempted to purchase a cheap imitation of the real thing? Remember that purse the sidewalk vendor tried to pass off as a designer one? You knew it wasn't real (no way, at that low price!) but you wondered if others would notice the subtle differences. It sure *looked* authentic. Ever buy an off-brand appliance only to call a repairman the next month? You have to admit the old saying is usually true—"You get what you pay for!"

God wants to bless you with peace that is superior to what the world offers. The world declares loudly through billboards and television that material things will bring you peace. Satan may tempt you with a relationship or choice that you know is not God's best. In the end, these empty promises will leave you anything but peaceful. God made you. He knows you from the inside out. He knows what will fill the empty spots in your heart and calm the storms that overwhelm you. Your Creator does not offer a cheap imitation. He is the real deal. Seek Him, and you will experience a peace that cannot be contained in words, a peace that passes understanding.

All Creatures Great and Small

But God chose the foolish things of this world to put the wise to shame.
He chose the weak things of this world to put the powerful to shame.
1 CORINTHIANS 1:27 CEV

God's economy is different from any other. The world places a high value on material wealth, physical strength, and outward beauty. Throughout God's Word, He makes it clear that this is not what He looks for in His creation. God looks at the heart. Perhaps in your family or among your coworkers, you feel small or unnoticed. Have you been passed over for a promotion? Are you unsure your contributions matter, perhaps a bit envious of those who seem to always outdo your best efforts?

The Bible is full of examples of "small" people who made a big impact. Zaccheus was small in stature but, upon meeting Christ, showed great character when he repaid those from whom he had stolen. Jesus even went home with Zaccheus! David was but a young shepherd boy when God chose him to slay the giant Goliath. God used a prostitute, a young boy with a sack lunch, and even a former murderer of Christians to do great things for the kingdom.

The next time you feel as if you are not making much of a difference at all, remember that your Creator uses the small to do great things. God sees your great value.

"These things I have spoken to you, so that in Me you may have peace. In the world you have tribulation, but take courage; I have overcome the world."
JOHN 16:33 NASB

God cannot give us a happiness and peace apart from Himself, because it is not there. There is no such thing.
C. S. LEWIS

Life gets so busy, God. Too busy. Let me take time to smell the roses today! You have created a world full of flowers and trees, amazing creatures such as the squirrels that dart across my yard and the birds whose songs provide a free concert if only I will slow down long enough to listen! Help me to slow down today. Amen.

God's Amazing Imagination

*Now the LORD God had formed out of the ground all the wild animals
and all the birds in the sky. He brought them to the man to see what he
would name them; and whatever the man called each living creature,
that was its name. So the man gave names to all the livestock,
the birds in the sky and all the wild animals.*
GENESIS 2:19–20 NIV

Like a scene from a movie, imagine it! God puts the finishing touches
on the animals. He paints the spots on the giraffe and stretches that
neck just a bit longer. He adds bright red warning signs to certain
snakes and insects. He leans back and smiles. "Ahhh, perfect," He
whispers to Himself, "Now, what shall each one be called?"

Oh, God could have named them Himself. His creativity
speaks for itself in the zebra's bold stripes and the howling of jungle
monkeys! No help was necessary in deciding upon their names. But
like the parent who allows a child to stir the cake batter or help
paint the garage, God gave this job to Adam. Imagine it! A parade
of animals in the Garden of Eden, each one uniquely crafted by
its Creator, passes by Adam. How long the first man must have
pondered some of those names—"butterfly," "hippopotamus," "boa
constrictor," "camel."

All it takes is a look around His world to know that God has
an amazing imagination! Each tree and flower, each animal and
insect bears intricate symmetry and beauty. One can almost see the
fingerprints of God upon His creation!

Fearfully and Wonderfully Made

*God created man in His own image, in the image of
God He created him; male and female He created them.*
GENESIS 1:27 NASB

There is nothing like a newborn baby to turn our thoughts toward
the Creator. Ten tiny fingers and toes, the first cry, sweet gurgles and
coos. . . . As many babies as one has seen, new life never ceases to
amaze. Humanity does not just exist. A big bang did not result in the
intricate detail called life. Nor did we evolve from apes. While they
are amazing creatures, they are not the creations God called "man"
and "woman." The Bible teaches that God made man different. He
made us in His image. Certainly a tiny baby is a reminder of the
miracle of life. But when was the last time you looked in the mirror?
Do you realize that you are *fearfully and wonderfully made*? It may have
been a few years back now, but God thought you up! He designed
you. The Bible says He knit you together in your mother's womb (see
Psalm 139:13). And He is pleased with His creation.

You are made in the image of the Lord Almighty. He loves you
immensely. You are more important to Him than the birds of the air
or the fish of the sea. You are His ultimate masterpiece. You are His
child.

All Your works shall praise You, O LORD,
And Your saints shall bless You.
PSALM 145:10 NKJV

Is your place a small place?
Tend it with care; He set you there.
Is your place a large place?
Guard it with care! He set you there.
Whate'er your place, it is not yours alone,
But His who set you there.
JOHN OXENHAM

God, remind me today that You do not make mistakes.
I am not intended to be like everyone else. I am designed
to be just the person You created me to be. Help me to use
my gifts and abilities to glorify You. Let me honor You
in all that I say and do today. Amen.

He Knows Our Hearts

"Indeed, the very hairs of your head are all numbered.
Do not fear; you are more valuable than many sparrows."
LUKE 12:7 NASB

Yolanda's classroom was a magical place. Education students from the local college were often sent to observe this phenomenal teacher. The test scores from Yolanda's class were always among the best in the school, and her students read at higher levels than expected for the second grade. But academic achievements aside, there was just something special about the way this educator interacted with her students. Yolanda knew her students. She knew more than just their names and the grades they had made on the last spelling test. She knew their hobbies, their preferences, little bits of trivia about their families. Yolanda knew the children's hearts.

God knows His children like that. When our Father looks down from heaven, He does not just see a group of human beings. He sees individuals. The Bible says He knows the number of hairs on your head. He knows your desires and dreams, your strengths and weaknesses. Talk to God today. Tell Him what you are worried about. Ask Him for help. He knows your heart, and He longs to spend time with you, His precious daughter.

All Things Wise and Wonderful

The law of the LORD is perfect,
refreshing the soul.
The statutes of the LORD are trustworthy,
making wise the simple.
PSALM 19:7 NIV

Have you been so thirsty that you simply couldn't wait to get a drink? As a drink of cold water satisfies a parched mouth, God's Word refreshes the soul that drinks deep of its truths. As a believer, you may not always understand why God's Word instructs you in a certain manner. In such times, trust that your loving heavenly Father has only your best interest at heart.

Wisdom is offered to the Christian who follows the ways of the Lord. Consider a true disciple of Jesus, perhaps an older person in your church fellowship that you would describe as wise. Undoubtedly, that individual's life story contains decision points between the ways of the world and God's ways. Choose to drink deep of the law of the Lord. Meditate on His scriptures. When your sin nature pulls you one direction but God's Word directs in another, you will never be disappointed if you choose God. His ways are perfect, and His law is designed to give you abundant life. As you grow in the wisdom of the Lord, you will find wonderful blessing. All things wise and wonderful. . .come from your Father.

Before a word is on my tongue
you, LORD, know it completely.
You hem me in behind and before,
and you lay your hand upon me.
Such knowledge is too wonderful for me,
too lofty for me to attain.
PSALM 139:4−6 NIV

The beauty of creation convinces me that the Creator
not only loves me, but He wants me to have the very best.
UNKNOWN

I find comfort, Lord, in knowing that You know me.
Even in my imperfection, You love me. You created me.
I am Yours. You see me as righteous because I have
accepted Your Son as my righteousness. You see me as
Your daughter, made in Your image. You long to spend
time with me. It feels good to be loved by You. Amen.

Light of the World

"You are the light of the world. A town built on a hill cannot be hidden. Neither do people light a lamp and put it under a bowl. Instead they put it on its stand, and it gives light to everyone in the house. In the same way, let your light shine before others, that they may see your good deeds and glorify your Father in heaven."
MATTHEW 5:14–16 NIV

Have you been outside in the country after dark? The stars illuminate the sky. They are big and bold and above all, they are bright! In the city, stars are not nearly as eye-catching. They are the same stars. It is pollution that clouds their brilliance. Are you a country star or a city star? It might seem like an odd question at first, but consider it.

Our charge as Christ followers is to be the light of the world! Bright light. Illuminating light. Difference-making light. Light that causes those around us to desire it for themselves. Light that shines in the darkness. Country star kind of light! Has the world polluted your light? With lives crowded with constant technology and trying to keep up with the latest trends, do we shine as brightly? Do we look different as believers, or do we blend in nicely with the world? Can others see your light? Is it bright. . .or is it dim? Jesus taught His followers that they were to be the light of the world. As His disciples in the twenty-first century, we are called to be this same light. Ask God to help you shine for Him.

The Songs of the Mountains

*"Seek the LORD while He may be found; Call upon Him while He is near.
Let the wicked forsake his way and the unrighteous man his thoughts;
And let him return to the LORD, And He will have compassion on him,
And to our God, For He will abundantly pardon. . . . So will My word
be which goes forth from My mouth; It will not return to Me empty,
Without accomplishing what I desire, And without succeeding in the matter
for which I sent it. For you will go out with joy And be led forth with peace;
The mountains and the hills will break forth into shouts of joy before you,
And all the trees of the field will clap their hands."*
ISAIAH 55:6—7; 11—12 NASB

There is a condition here. The songs of the mountains and rejoicing
of the trees are not without cause. The Lord is calling His people
back to Himself in this chapter of Isaiah. Have you strayed from
God? God's Word issues a distinct call back to Him. God is so
merciful! He stands ready to forgive. His grace is abundant, His love
unending. But verse 6 says *"Seek the LORD while He may be found; call upon
Him while He is near"* (NASB). The Bible tells of men who turned away
from God so long that their hearts were hardened. They were no
longer sensitive to the Lord's call. If you have begun to walk with the
world closer than you walk with the Lord, remember your heavenly
Father today. If there is a root of bitterness growing in your heart due
to unforgiveness, lay it before your God. Ask Him to draw you close
to Himself again. All creation will rejoice to see you return to your
Father's embrace! Imagine it: He says the mountains will burst forth
with song when His Word accomplishes this in your life. He says the
trees will clap their hands!

But the path of the righteous is like the light of dawn,
That shines brighter and brighter until the full day.
PROVERBS 4:18 NASB

It's your kindness, Lord, that leads us to repentance. Your favor,
Lord, is our desire. It's your beauty, Lord, that makes us stand
in silence. Your love, your love is better than life.
CHRIS TOMLIN

Jesus, light of the world, You are the way, the truth,
and the life. You are the Redeemer, my Savior, and amazingly
enough. . .You are also my friend. Give me the strength that it
takes to shine for You in the darkness of this world. It is easier
to dim my light. I long to shine it before others that they
might see my good works and glorify my God. Amen.

Creation's Daily Inspiration

For since the creation of the world God's invisible qualities—his eternal power and divine nature—have been clearly seen, being understood from what has been made, so that people are without excuse.
ROMANS 1:20 NIV

Creation tells of the Creator. It is that simple. Watch waves crash in on the shore. Feel the strength of a storm, the warmth of a sun so bright you cannot look upon it. These are living products of the Master's hands. You have, in looking upon His creation, glimpsed His majesty. In the power of creation, find God's strength. Examine an infant's tiny fingers. Breathe in deep the scents of lilacs and roses. Watch a baby deer begin to walk on wobbly legs. Taste the salt in your own tears as their release brings cleansing to your spirit. All of this did not just "come to be." It was designed, thought out, organized, and crafted. . .by your Father. Psalm 19 (NIV) says it like this: "The heavens declare the glory of God; the skies proclaim the work of his hands. Day after day they pour forth speech; night after night they reveal knowledge. They have no speech, they use no words; no sound is heard from them. Yet their voice goes out into all the earth, their words to the ends of the world." There is no denying the Creator. He has given you creation. Find Him in it today.

Be Still and Know That He Is God

He says, "Be still, and know that I am God;
I will be exalted among the nations,
I will be exalted in the earth."
The LORD Almighty is with us;
the God of Jacob is our fortress.
PSALM 46:10–11 NIV

Mary was a busy woman. No one who knew her would deny that! She was a wife, a mother, and also held down a full-time job in the business world. One day a frazzled coworker asked Mary how she did it all. "You never seem flustered. How do you do it?" The friend expected Mary to expose a special organization program or reveal that she had secretly hired a housekeeper and a cook! But it was nothing of the sort. Mary smiled and said, "I don't do it all. I learned a long time ago that I *can't* do it on my own. I have to rely on the Lord." Mary had discovered the secret of spending time with God. She took a few minutes each morning when the house was still quiet to go before her Creator God. Often Mary came to her prayer time with burdens and concerns. Sometimes her heart was filled with joy and thanksgiving. Regardless of her circumstances, she always thanked God for simply *being God*. She sat quietly before Him, listening, acknowledging His sovereignty and His presence in her life. Mary understood the meaning of being still and knowing that He is God.

For thus says the Lord GOD, the Holy One of Israel:
"In returning and rest you shall be saved;
In quietness and confidence shall be your strength."
ISAIAH 30:15 NKJV

See how nature—trees, flowers, grass—grows in silence;
see the stars, the moon, and the sun, how they move in
silence. . . . We need silence to be able to touch souls.
MOTHER TERESA

Lord, I am constantly pulled at to be busy, not still!
There are so many demands on my every day, my every
moment. But You ask me to be still. You are the one in
my life who truly wants me all to Yourself. You tell me to
be still and know that You are God. I know the rest will
fall into place. Teach me to be still, I pray. Amen.

He's Not Finished Yet

I thank my God every time I remember you. In all my prayers for all of you, I always pray with joy because of your partnership in the gospel from the first day until now, being confident of this, that he who began a good work in you will carry it on to completion until the day of Christ Jesus.
PHILIPPIANS 1:3–6 NIV

Do you feel that God is disappointed in you? Have you fallen into a bad habit or gone down a wrong path? Maybe it is a divorce or another damaged relationship in your life that causes you to believe God has given up on you. Nothing could be further from the truth. God loves you just as much today as He did when you were an innocent infant. He's not finished with you yet. Throughout your life, God will use circumstances and even disappointments to perfect you. Our heavenly Father never gives up on His children. Paul reminds the Philippians that God has begun a good work in them and that He will be faithful to complete it. When does Paul say that completion will be? He clearly states that it will not be until *the day of Christ Jesus.* Mankind is God's most prized creation. Even the angels are a little lower than mankind! Ask the Lord to help you as you seek to walk in His ways. He will be faithful. There will be times when you have regrets or need to choose to get back on the right road. But remember: God's not finished with you yet!

God Speaks through Creation

How many are your works, LORD!
In wisdom you made them all;
the earth is full of your creatures.
PSALM 104:24 NIV

The chirping of birds in springtime, the whisper of the wind as it blows through your hair on an early morning jog. . . . Have you considered these to be the very voice of the Creator? God speaks through His creation. Sometimes it may be the deep rumble of thunder followed by a flash of lightning, and other times the whimper of a warm puppy so small that you can hold him in one hand.

As you go throughout your day today, take notice of the world around you. Where do you see God? Where do you hear your Creator's voice? God reveals Himself to His children in personal ways. He desires an intimate, one-on-one relationship with each son and daughter. You may meet God on snowcapped mountains while skiing at amazing speed or you may find Him as you rest beside a quiet pond at the neighborhood park. The important thing is that you listen. Don't miss God in His creation. He wants to speak to you. He wants to show Himself real to you. He is the maker of all things, and He is reflected through His creation—if only we take time to notice.

The Lord God Made Them All

God saw all that he had made, and it was very good.
And there was evening, and there was morning—the sixth day.
GENESIS 1:31 NIV

There is a popular children's book that tells the story of a cricket who does not want to be a cricket. He admires the appearance and abilities of other animals and wishes that he could be more like them. Are we so different from the cricket?

It is a strong tendency of most women to compare ourselves with others. We wish we could be thinner or more organized, have curly hair instead of straight—or straight instead of curly! When was the last time you considered that the Lord God made you? He made you *just the way you are*. He knit you together in your mother's womb, weaving together in the secret place a perfect combination of traits and talents.

God made the world and everything in it. Genesis tells us that He then sat back and smiled. Well, not in so many words! But it says He saw His creation and was *pleased*. God is delighted with the details that make you who you are. Instead of wishing you were someone else, examine your abilities. You are not called to be what you are not, but you are called to make the most of what you are.

"My sheep hear My voice, and I know them, and they follow Me. And I give them eternal life, and they shall never perish; neither shall anyone snatch them out of My hand. My Father, who has given them to Me, is greater than all; and no one is able to snatch them out of My Father's hand."
JOHN 10:27–29 NKJV

Use the talents you possess—for the woods would be a very silent place if no birds sang except for the very best.
HENRY VAN DYKE

Father, sometimes I look for writing in the sky or listen for a booming voice from heaven. I search earnestly to know Your will and Your direction for my life. I love the times when I remember to rest quietly before You in Your creation. Nature has a way of calming my spirit and drawing me into Your presence. Speak to me through creation, God. Comfort my weary mind and give me direction, I pray. Amen.

Blessed Assurance

Blessed assurance, Jesus is mine!
Oh, what a foretaste of glory divine!
Heir of salvation, purchase of God,
Born of His Spirit, washed in His blood.

Refrain
This is my story, this is my song,
Praising my Savior all the day long;
This is my story, this is my song,
Praising my Savior all the day long.

Perfect submission, perfect delight,
Visions of rapture now burst on my sight;
Angels, descending, bring from above
Echoes of mercy, whispers of love.
Perfect submission, all is at rest,
I in my Savior am happy and blest,
Watching and waiting, looking above,
Filled with His goodness, lost in His love.
FANNY CROSBY, 1873

Fanny Crosby, a prolific hymn writer of the nineteenth century, possessed an amazing gift for writing poetry on the spot. Preachers often came to her with requests for new songs about specific subjects, and musicians sought her out for words to accompany the tunes they composed.

One day a close friend and amateur musician, Phoebe Knapp, came to Fanny. "Oh, Fanny, I have had a new melody racing through my mind for some time now, and I just can't think of anything else. Let me play it for you and perhaps you can help me with the words." Fanny knelt in prayer, seeking God for the words, then rose and declared, "Why, that music says, 'Blessed Assurance, Jesus is mine! O what a foretaste of glory divine. . . .'" The rest of the words soon flowed from her pen, and thus was born one of the most beloved hymns of all time.

Blessed Assurance

*In a wealthy home some utensils are made of gold and silver, and some
are made of wood and clay. The expensive utensils are used for special
occasions, and the cheap ones are for everyday use. If you keep yourself pure,
you will be a special utensil for honorable use. Your life will be clean,
and you will be ready for the Master to use you for every good work.*
2 TIMOTHY 2:20–21 NLT

Fanny Crosby, blind at six weeks of age, wrote the lyrics to "Blessed
Assurance" and is credited with more than eight thousand hymns.
When asked about her blindness she said, "It seemed intended by the
blessed providence of God that I should be blind all my life, and I
thank Him for the dispensation. If perfect earthly sight were offered
me tomorrow I would not accept it. I might not have sung hymns
to the praise of God if I had been distracted by the beautiful and
interesting things about me."

In today's culture it's easy to discount another's contribution to
society and to the kingdom of God. But every person has a specific
gift and purpose— to live our lives in a way that tells Jesus' story. No
matter what challenges you are facing in life, you can live above your
circumstances, just like Fanny Crosby chose to do. Live each day in
such a way that you tell the story of Jesus in all you say and do.

The Gift of Salvation

These things I have written to you who believe in the name of
the Son of God, that you may know that you have eternal life,
and that you may continue to believe in the name of the Son of God.
1 JOHN 5:13 NKJV

God created humankind for relationship with Him. From the time
Adam and Eve sinned (Genesis 3) to today, God's goal has been to
restore His relationship with His children. Through the birth, death,
burial, and resurrection of His only Son, Jesus, He provided us a
way back to Him. Jesus laid down His life and trusted God to raise
Him up again. Through Christ's obedience, He built a bridge for us
to cross spiritually between heaven and earth, from our souls to the
throne room of God, to live each day with our heavenly Father.

The greatest gift ever given—or ever received—is our salvation.
It allows us to step into God's presence from death to life. Through
Jesus Christ, we have assurance that we can spend this life and all
eternity in His presence. Hallelujah!

"The LORD is my strength and song,
And He has become my salvation;
He is my God, and I will praise Him;
My father's God, and I will exalt Him."
EXODUS 15:2 NKJV

Spread love everywhere you go: First of all in your own house. . .
let no one ever come to you without leaving better and happier.
Be the living expression of God's kindness; kindness in your face,
kindness in your eyes, kindness in your smile, kindness.
MOTHER TERESA

Jesus, thank You for the gift of salvation. I ask that You
forgive me of every sin in my life. Wash me clean and bury
the things in my past that separated me from You and from
my heavenly Father. I ask for a fresh start today. I choose
God's will and His ways for my life. I surrender my life to You.
Give me a clean heart and fill me with Your Spirit today. Amen.

Bought at a Price

"Again, the kingdom of heaven is like a merchant seeking
beautiful pearls, who, when he had found one pearl of
great price, went and sold all that he had and bought it."
MATTHEW 13:45–46 NKJV

Everything comes with a price. Each day we make dozens of decisions based on the cost. Sometimes it's a financial cost, but it could also be the cost of relationships, health, or faith. Jesus counted the cost. Jesus willingly gave away His place in heaven, stepped down, and became a man, confined to a body that would ultimately experience a painful death. He submitted His own will and did the will of the heavenly Father by laying down His life. He gave a life that was only His to give so that all could experience eternal life. He paid an unimaginable price so that every man, woman, and child could receive salvation.

It cost the Father and the Son separation from one another while Jesus hung on the cross, bearing every sin that would ever be sinned. It was the highest price that could have been paid—and yet God considered each person worth it all. Every moment of pain and humiliation, the Father and Son endured for a relationship with God's beloved creation. You are valuable and considered a pearl of great price—a price God was willing to pay.

Washed in His Blood

Then He took the cup, and gave thanks, and said, "Take this and divide it among yourselves; for I say to you, I will not drink of the fruit of the vine until the kingdom of God comes." And He took bread, gave thanks and broke it, and gave it to them, saying, "This is My body which is given for you; do this in remembrance of Me." Likewise He also took the cup after supper, saying, "This cup is the new covenant in My blood, which is shed for you."
LUKE 22:17–21 NKJV

A hemopurifier is a machine that works kind of like a dialysis machine. It filters blood using thin fibers to trap and eliminate viruses from the blood of infected patients. A hemopurifier can treat many illnesses by drawing blood from the individual, into a tube, through the machine, and then sending it back into the person's body. Sin is the deadly disease that infected all of creation on the day that Adam and Eve chose to disobey God. When Jesus gave His life, His blood provided the ultimate sacrifice. His sinless life was poured out in exchange for the sin-stained lives of anyone who willingly accepts Jesus Christ as the Lord and Savior of their life. Much like the hemopurifier works on a physical body, spiritually, Jesus' blood purified the hearts of believers— eradicating the disease of sin.

In God's eyes an exchange was made; a transfusion occurred. We become clean and righteous in God's sight through the washing of the blood of Jesus. Through His blood we can stand in the presence of God pure and righteous because Jesus poured His life out for ours.

You surely know that your body is a temple where the
Holy Spirit lives. The Spirit is in you and is a gift from God.
You are no longer your own. God paid a great price for you.
So use your body to honor God.
1 CORINTHIANS 6:19–20 CEV

God just doesn't throw a life preserver to a drowning person.
He goes to the bottom of the sea and pulls a corpse from
the bottom of the sea, takes him up on the bank, breathes
into him the breath of life, and makes him alive.
R. C. SPROUL

Lord, You paid a great price for my salvation. You gave up
your throne to become a man and live Your life among us.
You chose to do the Father's will to bridge the gap between
heaven and earth so that I might know God's great love and
experience eternal life. You humiliated Yourself and became
sin so that I might go free instead of bearing the penalty of
my own sin. Thank You for Your willingness to give Your
life for mine. Help me live my life pleasing to You. Amen.

Walking in His Footsteps

For I have not spoken on My own authority; but the Father who sent Me gave Me a command, what I should say and what I should speak. And I know that His command is everlasting life. Therefore, whatever I speak, just as the Father has told Me, so I speak."
JOHN 12:49–50 NKJV

A four-year-old girl follows her grandfather into the field as he plants corn. He takes the end of a shovel and drops it into the loosely tilled soil then tosses several seeds of corn into the hole. The little girl squats down behind him, pokes her little finger into the dirt, and drops a single kernel of corn into the hole. Children learn by mimicking the actions of adults. The same is true in spiritual growth. Jesus said, "Follow Me!"

Christ came to the earth to live a life pleasing to the Father. He led the way by example, and many of those examples are recorded in the Bible. When most adults would run children off, Jesus said, "Let the children come to Me." When others wanted to stone the woman caught in adultery, Jesus said, "He who is without sin, cast the first stone." When you aren't certain of what you should do, you can look to the life of Jesus. He chose to follow the will of the Father. He made decisions and took actions that were pleasing in His Father's sight. Take Jesus at His words: "Follow Me!"

My Confidence in Christ

Such is the confidence that we have through Christ toward God.
Not that we are sufficient in ourselves to claim anything
as coming from us, but our sufficiency is from God.
2 CORINTHIANS 3:4–5 ESV

The book of Esther tells a story of a young woman who probably had every opportunity to believe God had forgotten her. She had been orphaned as a child, adopted and raised by her cousin, and living as an exile in a foreign land. Esther's confidence in God could very easily have been shaken. She could have cast her confidence aside and believed what her eyes told her about the condition of God's heart toward His people. But she continued to trust God and grow in relationship with Him. Through her determination to hold tight to God, in His timing she became the key He used to save the very lives of her people. In spite of her hidden nationality, Esther had found favor with the king and had been chosen as his queen. She realized it was nothing she had done, but something the Lord had done on her behalf. When you trust God for the outcome of a situation you're facing, you can choose His will and His way. You can remain confident that He will provide you with whatever you need—and the ability to do whatever He has asked you to do when the time comes. Refuse to cast your confidence aside. Hold fast to God and His promises.

Guide my steps by your word,
so I will not be overcome by evil.
PSALM 119:133 NLT

To take up the cross of Christ is no great action done
once for all; it consists in the continual practice
of small duties which are distasteful to us.
JOHN HENRY NEWMAN

Lord, I get so lost sometimes when I forget that I am to
follow instead of lead. I want to know where I am going.
Forgive me when I step out ahead of You and take my own
path. Give me wisdom to recognize when I have done that.
I want to live each day in Your footsteps, going the distance
as I follow You. Help me to be a good follower,
as You lead me every day. Amen.

Whispers of Love

"It is the Spirit who gives life; the flesh is no help at all. The words that I have spoken to you are spirit and life."
JOHN 6:63 ESV

Prayer is an exchange, a conversation often uttered in whispers, between God and His child. There are countless examples in the Bible of whispers from God providing direction and instruction. God called to Moses from a burning bush in the desert and gave him the assignment of his life (see Exodus 3). God whispered to Samuel while he was just a child in the middle of the night to give him a warning of things to come in the prophet Eli's house (see 1 Samuel 3). And Jesus spoke to Saul, who soon became Paul, asking Saul why he was persecuting Him (see Acts 22). In the midst of this confrontation, one of the greatest persecutors of the church became a Christian. As you build a relationship with God and grow in knowing His voice, you learn to follow His lead. There are no perfect prayers or right ways of talking to God. He is ready and willing to hear your heart and answer the big and small questions in life. His gentle nudges and whispers of love provide instruction in reply to the questions you've asked. As you listen, you will find the direction you need to live your life in a way that pleases Him.

Jesus Is My Song

*Sing hymns instead of drinking songs! Sing songs from your heart
to Christ. Sing praises over everything, any excuse for a song
to God the Father in the name of our Master, Jesus Christ.*
EPHESIANS 5:19–20 MSG

Writers, composers, singers—all have tried to capture the very
music that speaks to the soul of humankind. But when your soul is
connected to God through acceptance of Jesus Christ, Jesus becomes
your very song. A heart inhabited by Jesus cries out praise and
adoration for the gift of salvation. We may struggle to understand
His sacrifice, but we know He gave up His position in heaven
to come to earth to lay down His very life into the hands of men
who hated Him. When you think of all He gave up to secure our
salvation, it's nearly impossible to believe. He accepted death so that
we could have life. He gave us peace instead of chaos. He made a way
for us to experience faith in place of fear. He became the bridge that
connects us to the Father, so that we could speak to the Father and
come before His throne without sin. His willingness to give Himself
for you is the reason your soul can overflow with praise and live a life
where Jesus really is your song!

"Behold, God is my salvation,
I will trust and not be afraid;
For the LORD GOD is my strength and song,
And He has become my salvation."
ISAIAH 12:2 NASB

It may seem a little old-fashioned, always to begin one's
work with prayer, but I never undertake a hymn without
first asking the good Lord to be my inspiration.
FANNY CROSBY

Heavenly Father, let my life be a song of praise to You.
May Your Holy Spirit, living in me, help me to express
praise to You. I pray that all I do and all I say bring pleasure
to You. I am fearfully and wonderfully made in Your image.
I desire for my life to light the way for others to know You.
Thank You for the joy of knowing You. Thank You
for loving me unconditionally. Amen.

My Hope of Heaven

For we know that when this earthly tent we live in is taken down (that is, when we die and leave this earthly body), we will have a house in heaven, an eternal body made for us by God himself and not by human hands.
2 CORINTHIANS 5:1 NLT

God created us humans as eternal beings; time does not stop with physical death. Often when a loved one dies, the grieving family members turn their thoughts to heaven and God's promise of eternal life. It gives a peace knowing that someday they will see them again and be united for eternity in heaven. Christian apologist and writer C. S. Lewis said, "To enter heaven is to become more human than you ever succeeded in being on earth; to enter hell, is to be banished from humanity." Paul compares the Christian life to a race, with the winner taking the prize of eternal life (Philippians 3:14). As believers, our focus should not be on the things of this life—but on our future with Jesus Christ. Paul encourages believers to live for the heavenly prize rather than the rewards on earth. Heaven is the final destination for every person who accepts Christ and lives for Him, and God desires for all to know Him. This life is short in comparison to all eternity, but how we choose to live it makes an impact on those around us. We can live each day with God's blessing and favor, knowing that we bring pleasure to Him in our thoughts, feelings, and behavior.

Angels Surround Me

Do not neglect to show hospitality to strangers,
for by this some have entertained angels without knowing it.
HEBREWS 13:2 NASB

Songs have been written and stories have been told since the beginning of time, recording the influence of God's angels. Maybe you have even personally felt a supernatural intervention in your own life or experienced a visit from someone that you thought might have been an angel. The Bible is full of stories of angelic encounters. Angels protected Daniel's very life in the lions' den by shutting the hungry beasts' mouths (Daniel 6:22). An angel announced the promise of children to their parents: Abraham and Sarah, Zechariah (John was the baby!), and Elizabeth, and Joseph and Mary. Angels warned Lot of the pending destruction of Sodom and Gomorrah and Joseph of Herod's plan to kill the baby Jesus (Matthew 2:13). Still today stories are shared of divine intervention in the lives of God's people. Miraculous stories of those who supernaturally avoided tragedy or survived a terrible ordeal much like the story of Paul's escape from prison at the hand of His angel (Acts 12:1—9).

God's Word is very clear that angels are sent to minister to God's children. They often provide protection, intervention, encouragement, or instruction. They are not to be worshipped, like God, but to be received as messengers from God's throne, doing the Lord's good pleasure on our behalf.

No evil will befall you,
Nor will any plague come near your tent.
For He will give His angels charge concerning you,
To guard you in all your ways.
They will bear you up in their hands,
That you do not strike your foot against a stone.
PSALM 91:10—12 NASB

Why should my heart be fixed where my home is not?
Heaven is my home; God in Christ is all my happiness:
and where my treasure is, there my heart should be.
MARGARET CHARLTON BAXTER

Lord, there are times in my life that I have experienced
supernatural intervention—times I may not have even
recognized it. Thank You for all the times that You have
sent Your messengers—Your angels in my life. There are
many times, unknown to me, that they have shielded me
from the enemy or brought answers to my prayers.
Thank You! Amen.

Watching and Waiting

"You will keep him in perfect peace,
Whose mind is stayed on You,
Because he trusts in You."
ISAIAH 26:3 NKJV

For nine long months, an expectant mother awaits the arrival of her baby. Physical, mental, and emotional preparations all help her focus on the main thing: the baby growing inside her womb. She has a focal point to a sometimes all-consuming goal: to welcome the baby into the world. As Christians, we have another goal in mind—to focus on Jesus Christ and eagerly await His return. This world is temporary; heaven is the final destination for all who have accepted Christ as their Lord and Savior. This life seems very real—it's tangible. The minutes tick by, and we can easily become consumed by living in the moment. Challenges, problems, difficulties, and hardships can be overwhelming, drawing all our attention to this life on earth. The pressures can cause distraction, causing us take our eyes off the focal point, eventually losing sight of the big picture. The Bible tells believers to watch and wait for the time when Christ calls them home. Today, focus on the strength that comes from the one and only Savior of the world. How do we cultivate an expectant heart? By reading the Bible, spending time in prayer, and drawing strength from fellowship with other believers. Come, Lord Jesus, come!

Jesus Is My Resting Place

> *"Peace I leave with you; my peace I give to you.
> Not as the world gives do I give to you. Let not
> your hearts be troubled, neither let them be afraid."*
> JOHN 14:27 ESV

The world moves at a fast pace. Schedules are full, and most people are busier than ever. The chaos of family relationships, ongoing economic concerns, and a host of other issues today lend to frustrations and constant interruptions. It's easy to fall into the trap of worry in your life and in the lives of friends and family. It leaves little time for rest and relaxation.

Just as a time of rest for your physical body is vital to your health, rest for your spirit is also important. The worries and concerns of life can weigh heavy sometimes, but Jesus encourages us to give our concerns to Him. So imagine packing up all your worries, putting them in a suitcase, and shipping them off to Him. He will never return to sender. The Prince of Peace makes His peace available to everyone who believes in Him (Isaiah 9:6; John 14:27). When you make time for quiet moments with your Savior, His peace provides a rest for your soul that allows you the assurance you can remain steadfast and secure in the midst of the most difficult circumstances. When your soul is anchored in Him, He becomes the very source of peace.

"Come to Me, all you who labor and are heavy laden, and I will give you rest. Take My yoke upon you and learn from Me, for I am gentle and lowly in heart, and you will find rest for your souls."
MATTHEW 11:28–29 NKJV

Thou hast created us for Thyself,
and our hearts are restless until they rest in Thee.
SAINT AUGUSTINE

Jesus, my world moves at a fast pace every day. You are my place of peace. When the world crowds in and I can't find rest, please gently remind me to take a breath and get away to a place where I can spend time with You. Wash me in a shower of Your presence and infuse me with Your strength. Help me to remember I can't do this on my own—and I don't have to. Today I'm inviting You to do my life with me. Amen.

Filled with His Goodness

Every good gift and every perfect gift is from above,
and comes down from the Father of lights,
with whom there is no variation or shadow of turning.
JAMES 1:17 NKJV

When a witness in a court case gives an account of what he saw, he provides a record of what was said and done. When we share our stories of God's miraculous intervention in our lives, we're testifying on God's behalf much like a witness in a court of law. God encourages each generation to tell the next generation of His miraculous intervention in the lives of His people. The Bible is full of stories of how God delivered His people from the hands of their enemies, gave them water in the desert, opened the Red Sea so they could cross on dry land, and brought them into the Promised Land. During Jesus' time on the earth He healed the sick, raised the dead, and showered those who would receive Him with His Father's goodness—mercy and grace. God stories are still powerful today. When someone shares the story of God's goodness in his or her life, it builds faith, increases hope, removes limits, and inspires listeners to believe that what God can do for one—He will do for another. God's sons and daughters are created in His image—to reflect His likeness. God is everything good, and so His children are also filled with His goodness. Share His mercy, goodness, and love with the lives of those He brings into your life today.

Lost in His Love

As high as heaven is over the earth,
so strong is his love to those who fear him.
And as far as sunrise is from sunset,
he has separated us from our sins.
As parents feel for their children,
GOD feels for those who fear him.
He knows us inside and out,
keeps in mind that we're made of mud.
PSALM 103:11–14 MSG

God is love, and that love should influence every area of a Christian's life. Love is who God is—love is His very nature. God's love is more than a mother loves a child or a husband loves a wife. No matter how you try to imagine it or measure it—there is no end to the depths of God's love for you. Within our relationship with God there are times when it seems that God stands at a distance, longing for us to return His love by giving our all back to Him. It's when we give ourselves fully and completely to His will and plan for our lives that we can know His love completely. As we come to God as His child and totally trust Him, it's then that we can find His deepest love for us, like a child who melts into her father's arms. The greatest experience a child of God can have is to become forever lost—safe and secure in His immeasurable, infinite, unending love.

Praising My Savior All the Day Long

Bless the LORD, O my soul, and all that is within me,
bless his holy name! Bless the LORD, O my soul,
and forget not all his benefits, who forgives all your iniquity,
who heals all your diseases, who redeems your life from the pit,
who crowns you with steadfast love and mercy, who satisfies you
with good so that your youth is renewed like the eagle's.
PSALM 103:1—5 ESV

King David was a songwriter and a worshipper of the Lord who wrote seventy-plus psalms credited to him in the Bible. Through these words of worship and praise, King David provides an open book of the thoughts, feelings, and intentions of his heart toward his Lord. Through failure and triumph, tragedy and great success, he lived life in praise to God. And there's much we can learn from the words King David penned. Mankind was created to praise God (Isaiah 43:7; Matthew 21:16). Adam and Eve's disobedience and sin severed a perfect relationship between the Creator and His creation. Praise helps to restore a believer's relationship with God. The Creator resides in the praises of His people (Psalm 22:3). Praise silences the enemy, builds faith in the believer, and opens the heart to God. Praise isn't a single act you do, but a continual flow from the heart of man to God. Take time to praise the Lord by telling Him how you feel about Him. Let the heart of thanksgiving flow through you today.

Enter His gates with thanksgiving
And His courts with praise.
Give thanks to Him, bless His name.
PSALM 100:4 NASB

In almost everything that touches our everyday life on earth,
God is pleased when we're pleased. He wills that we be as free as
birds to soar and sing our Maker's praise without anxiety.
A. W. TOZER

Lord, my greatest desire is to please You. You gave me eternal
life, and I want to give my life back to You each day. You
consider me worthy of the greatest sacrifice by giving Your
life for mine. I praise You. You are the ultimate example of
selflessness and love. I will lift my voice in praise to
You all of my days. Amen.

Sweet Hour of Prayer

Sweet hour of prayer! Sweet hour of prayer!
That calls me from a world of care,
And bids me at my Father's throne
Make all my wants and wishes known.
In seasons of distress and grief,
My soul has often found relief
And oft escaped the tempter's snare
By thy return, sweet hour of prayer!

Sweet hour of prayer! Sweet hour of prayer!
The joys I feel, the bliss I share,
Of those whose anxious spirits burn
With strong desires for thy return!
With such I hasten to the place
Where God my Savior shows His face,
And gladly take my station there,
And wait for thee, sweet hour of prayer!

Sweet hour of prayer! Sweet hour of prayer!
May I thy consolation share,
Till, from Mount Pisgah's lofty height,
I view my home and take my flight:
This robe of flesh I'll drop and rise
To seize the everlasting prize;
And shout, while passing through the air,
Farewell, farewell, sweet hour of prayer!

WILLIAM WALFORD, 1845

Little is known of William Walford, author of "Sweet Hour of Prayer," apart from the fact that he was a blind whittler who occasionally filled the pulpit of his rural English church and had committed most of the Bible to memory. One day Thomas Salmon, an American pastor serving in England, visited William in his home. The blind man asked Thomas to transcribe the words of a poem he had composed in his head. Thomas took the words back to America with him and had them published in a New York newspaper. Fifteen years later William Bradbury, a composer from New York, wrote the tune that is usually associated with the song. "Sweet Hour of Prayer" slowly gained in popularity and was published in a Methodist hymnal for the first time in 1878.

Sweet Hour of Prayer

The apostles [sent out as missionaries] came back and gathered together
to Jesus, and told Him all that they had done and taught. And He said
to them, [As for you] come away by yourselves to a deserted place,
and rest a while—for many were [continually] coming and going.
MARK 6:30–31 AMP

Women are natural nurturers, always looking to fill the needs of others. Spending seemingly hour after hour *doing*—and perhaps hardly ever just *being*—we often put ourselves last on the list. Thank God for Jesus who understands that amid the world's hectic pace, we daughters of the King need time to re-center, refuel, and retool. The nurturers need to be nurtured.

At Jesus' invitation in Mark 6:31, we are called to pull ourselves away from the people and things clamoring for our attention. To turn away from the outside world and be refilled in the inner. To bring Jesus, not just our pleas and petitions, but our very presence—heart, body, mind, and soul—in prayer.

It doesn't matter what time of day it is. It doesn't matter what's on the to-do list. What matters is setting yourself down and allowing Christ to lift you up. It's time to disconnect the phone, turn off the TV, and shut the door. Take a moment—or more—each day to come away, alone with Jesus, to a deserted place, remembering that the longer a lady lingers, prayerfully present, the sweeter the sense of the Savior.

World of Care

He raised us up together with Him and made us sit down together
[giving us joint seating with Him] in the heavenly sphere [by virtue
of our being] in Christ Jesus (the Messiah, the Anointed One).
EPHESIANS 2:6 AMP

The gravity of this world so pulls at us earthlings that at times it's hard to shrug off the problems of today and reach the heavenlies in Christ. This is especially true for those of us who are determined to fix all problems, such is our compassion for our loved ones. Yet, through the blessing of prayer, Christ calls His sisters to rise up, take His hand, and boldly approach God.

As little children, with hearts full of forgiveness and love for ourselves and others, we can shake off our worries, rise above the fray, and come before God's throne. It is there our names are written (see Luke 10:20) and our citizenship resides (see Philippians 3:20). It is the store place of treasures (see Luke 12:33) and the outlet of blessings (see John 3:27). It is where Christ now sits at the right hand of God (see Hebrews 8:1) and stands with God's people before God Himself.

God's throne is the home of our desires, where we feel the most valued and loved, and where all hope lies (see Colossians 1:5). There we receive our calling, guidance, and plan for the day, week, month, and life. An ultimate great escape from a world of care, the heavenlies are not a place to enjoy someday, but a place to spend time in every day.

"When you pray, go into your inner room, close your door and pray to your Father who is in secret, and your Father who sees what is done in secret will reward you."
MATTHEW 6:6 NASB

What is heaven, but to be with God, to dwell with him, to realize that God is mine, and I am His?
CHARLES SPURGEON

Lord, I come to seek Your face, to rest in Your presence. Fill me with Your love and compassion. Give me the energy to do all You have called me to do. Quiet my mind so that I can focus on You and only You. For without You, Jesus, without Your love, power, and guidance, I am lost. I desire You like no other. And now, here, in this place, abiding in You, I have everything I need.

Wants and Wishes

Keep on asking and it will be given you; keep on seeking and you will find;
keep on knocking [reverently] and [the door] will be opened to you.
For everyone who keeps on asking receives; and he who keeps on seeking finds;
and to him who keeps on knocking, [the door] will be opened.
MATTHEW 7:7–8 AMP

Prayer is our way of making all our wants and wishes known to God the Father—the Master Nurturer. It doesn't matter what words we use, or if we merely groan or softly sigh, because God already knows the desires of our hearts. His all-seeing presence shines its light into the very corners of your being. His all-knowingness discerns what desires are in line with His and what wishes are outside of His will. Either way, God is eager and absolutely able to answer the prayer of you, His darling daughter. But you must be patient, for His response will come in His own time.

So Jesus urges us to never become discouraged but simply keep on asking, keep on seeking, and keep on knocking. Like the persistent widow, we're told not to lose heart, not to give up. For God, a generous and loving Father, will not fail to bring what is best to His daughters. And here is where our tenacity pays off. For she who is persistent in her prayer and confident in the love and power of her Almighty Father will have her godly desires fulfilled—all to His glory. That's a power-filled promise!

Relief of Grief

Then they cry out to the LORD in their trouble,
And He brings them out of their distresses.
He calms the storm, so that its waves are still.
Then they are glad because they are quiet;
So He guides them to their desired haven.
PSALM 107:28–30 NKJV

Life is full of unexpected twists and turns. Just when we think we have it all figured out and our strategies for navigating the world are in place, something unforeseen happens, sending carefully laid plans careening out of control, if not blowing them out of the water completely. Such surprises come in a variety of forms and result in a myriad of emotions. Any loss—of a job, a romance, a loved one, financial security—can cause us deep distress and grief. Thank God there is a great big Someone who can provide relief to the wounded heart, mind, body, and soul.

By running to God, focusing on Christ, and surrendering to the Spirit, we can find an infinite supply of healing and comfort. God gives the hurting strength to weather the storm. Pouring out the overwhelming pain and grief, our tears are captured in Christ's capable hands. The Comforter rushes in, a balm to the soul. When all the dust settles and a new normalcy takes over, we realize that in the midst of our loss, we can learn a lesson: no matter what happens, there will always be a refuge where our grief turns to joy, tears to laughter, heartache to healing, weakness to strength, turmoil to peace.

Answer me when I call, O God of my righteousness!
You have relieved me in my distress;
Be gracious to me and hear my prayer.
PSALM 4:1 NASB

Prayer is not so much the means whereby
God's will is bent to man's desires, as it is that
whereby man's will is bent to God's desires.
CHARLES BENT

Lord, Your Word says that You will energize me and create
in me the power and desire to do Your will. You have given
me so much that I want my will to match Yours. I want to
please You in all I say and do. Open my ears, heart, mind,
and spirit to Your Word in prayer. Make Your message
clear so that I can do all that pleases You.

Tempter's Snare

No temptation has overtaken you except such as is common to man;
but God is faithful, who will not allow you to be tempted beyond
what you are able, but with the temptation will also make
the way of escape, that you may be able to bear it.
1 CORINTHIANS 10:13 NKJV

We face a myriad of temptations every day—the temptation to get the last word in; to share a juicy piece of gossip; to say "I told you so"; to finish off that second piece of cake; to spend money on a dress, shoes, or a purse we really can't afford. Some temptations seem rather harmless. But some can sap the joy out of loved ones. And others can forever alter the world, as proven by Eve. Because she yielded to her own desires instead of God's, the first female became the catalyst for an immense Fall. So where can we turn in times of temptation? To God and His Word.

Versed and immersed in scripture, we can discern the difference between the Shepherd's voice and that of the devil. Through memorization of the Word, we, like Jesus when tempted in the desert, can use God's Word to fight off the dark one's advances. And by abiding in Christ and prayer, we can access the power to withstand anything.

Then forearmed and forewarned, we need merely keep our spiritual eyes open. For in all temptations, God provides a way of escape. Our job? To find it and, once there, breathe in the open air.

Joys and Bliss

*[For it is He] Who rescued and saved us from such a perilous death,
and He will still rescue and save us; in and on Him we have set our
hope (our joyful and confident expectation) that He will again deliver
us [from danger and destruction and draw us to Himself].*
2 CORINTHIANS 1:10 AMP

The media constantly feeds the message that in order to be happy, we
need to look younger, sexier, and more fashionable. In other words,
"You will never be good enough 'as is.' " Unfortunately, if we're
focused on the world's view of all that we are not, depression and
despondency are bound to set in.

But as Christians, we have a friend named Jesus, a man with a
history of rescuing His people from the world and its strictures. As
He was with Shadrach, Meshach, and Abednego, Christ is with His
followers even in the fire, enabling us to not only escape the furnace,
but to do so with neither singe nor smell of smoke. He is and will
forever be the eternal, *true* lifesaver of all who believe. What joy this
fact gives to us, women of the way who listen to *His* message *alone*!

Unlike happiness, which depends on circumstances, this joy in
Christ is available to God's daughter who knows there's only one
person to please—God Himself. As we continually, confidently, and
expectantly walk with Christ, we step around the world's dangerous
pitfalls and find overwhelming joy, a spring that drenches our core so
we can bless others.

Let all those who take refuge and put their trust in You rejoice;
let them ever sing and shout for joy, because You make a covering
over them and defend them; let those also who love Your
name be joyful in You and be in high spirits.
PSALM 5:11 AMP

Prayer covers the whole of man's life. There is no thought,
feeling, yearning, or desire, however low, trifling, or vulgar
we may deem it, which if it affects our real interest or happiness,
we may not lay before God and be sure of sympathy.
HENRY WARD BEECHER

Jesus, I am overwhelmed with joy, knowing that as I abide
in You, nothing can move me. You keep me safe from gossip,
loss, sorrow, backbiting, covetousness, and other weapons of
destruction. In Your presence I long to remain, for in You alone
do I live, move, and have my being. Teach me to pray You
into me. Joyful am I as I stand in Your presence.

Savior's Face

If My people, who are called by My name, shall humble themselves,
pray, seek, crave, and require of necessity My face. . .then will
I hear from heaven, forgive their sin, and heal their land.
2 CHRONICLES 7:14 AMP

Sometimes we simply want to be loved. God is the same way. So He asks us to seek His face. "Seeking His face" means entering God's presence with no other agenda but to spend time with Him. In these moments, we're not asking Him to carry our burdens. We're not asking for Him to come to our rescue. And we're not asking Him to do something for us. It is merely His daughter humbling herself and coming to Him to "pray, seek, crave, and require" His face out of *her* necessity.

Oftentimes a child seeks out her mother's presence for no other reason than wanting to be with her. Her arms open wide as soon as Mommy walks into the room. Out of a need that is all encompassing, she craves her mother's face, presence, love, and warmth. And the child has no rest until she reaches her, perhaps even crying until Mommy bends down, scoops her up, and enfolds her in her arms, sharing her warmth with the child she has borne.

God would have us—His daughters—seek His face and desire His presence in the same way a child craves that of her loving mother. All we need to do is pray, seek, and crave His face, and God's response will be swift and wondrous as He leans down from heaven, opens His arms, and scoops us into His all-loving presence.

Waiting Station

---

*Let be and be still, and know
(recognize and understand) that I am God.*
PSALM 46:10 AMP

Tense from the stress of housework, homework, career, kids, and romance, you might become impatient to get into the presence of Christ. As you try to settle yourself, it's difficult to be still (physically and mentally) when there's so much to be done. So you reach for the Bible—the key to rising above all the noise of life—your gateway to that one-on-One focus on the Father Himself.

Soaking in the scriptures, you find your mind and soul calming, bringing your heart closer and closer to Father God's. Making the Word your own, you call on Jesus, realizing the humor in the fact that He really doesn't need to be called because He's been right next to you all along. It's just that, until then, you hadn't *recognized* Him there.

As your tension falls away, your physical eyes close and spiritual eyes open. As you seek the Savior's face, your will fades and becomes one with His. Silent and still, you experience His unconditional love and acceptance. At last, fully in His presence, you're prompted into prayer—that sweet communication, that privileged link from daughter to Father in the stillness and silence of His kingdom. Amen.

"Can a woman forget her nursing child,
And not have compassion on the son of her womb?
Surely they may forget, yet I will not forget you."
ISAIAH 49:15 NKJV

Those who know God the best are the richest and most
powerful in prayer. Little acquaintance with God, and strangeness
and coldness to Him, make prayer a rare and feeble thing.
E. M. BOUNDS

Lord, I come seeking Your face today—nothing more,
nothing less. I have no petitions, no complaints, no pleas.
I merely crave Your presence, Your strength, and Your peace.
I want to rest quietly here with You, feeling Your arms
around me and allowing Your love to fill me up. Here,
with You, I am content to simply be. There is
nothing to do—there is merely You.

Winged Petition

*Do not fret or have any anxiety about anything, but in every circumstance
and in everything, by prayer and petition (definite requests),
with thanksgiving, continue to make your wants known to God.*
PHILIPPIANS 4:6 AMP

Often we may not really know what to request of God until we have
worked through the problem, pouring out our heart to the Lord in
prayer. We women sometimes need to "talk it out" in order to clear
our minds before we can even begin to put words to our pleas.

Consider childless Hannah who went to the temple in "deep
anguish" and prayed to the Lord, "weeping bitterly" (1 Samuel 1:10
NIV). At the end of her emptying process (prayer), she asked God for
a son (petition), promising to give him back to the Lord if her request
was answered. Having given over her burden and found new hope
with her plea, she went on her way in peace, "her face. . .no longer
downcast" (1 Samuel 1:18 NIV). And God gave her a son.

Out of our poured-out prayers come poignant petitions. Once
they are delivered, we can allow our faith to hold us up as we leave
our sorrows and requests with our Friend and Father and find peace
and direction. If our petition is in accordance with God's will, He
will, in His time, grant our desires.

Engaged in Waiting

Be still and rest in the Lord; wait for
Him and patiently lean yourself upon Him.
PSALM 37:7 AMP

In this I-want-it-now society, patience seems to be on a steady decline. But staying power is just what the Lord wants His daughters to have. Martin Luther said that, in Hebrew, Psalm 37:7 meant " 'Be silent in God and let Him mould thee.' Keep still, and He will mould thee to the right shape."

But how do we "keep still"? By not tapping our toes in impatience. By focusing on God's will, not our own agenda. By not running ahead of God or trying to manipulate circumstances to gain what we believe we deserve.

God wants His daughters to confidently walk in faith, knowing that He will deliver *in His time*, according to His will, and always remains true to His word. If we trust in God, we have every right to expect Him to bless us, as did the lame man who "paid attention. . . expecting that he was going to get something" (Acts 3:5 AMP) and was healed! It's persistent expectation that God looks kindly upon.

Our game plan should be to continually rest in God and wait, leaning on Him at every misstep, tragedy, and heartache, knowing that no matter what happens, we may confidently expect to "see the goodness of the LORD in the land of the living" (Psalm 27:13 NKJV). Such patience and faith is amply rewarded by the God who constantly looks to find and abundantly bless His daughters.

I waited patiently for the LORD;
And He inclined to me and heard my cry.
PSALM 40:1 NASB

Never was a faithful prayer lost. Some prayers have a
longer voyage than others, but then they return with
their richer landing at last, so that the praying soul
is a gainer by waiting for an answer.
WILLIAM GURNALL

I am confidently and expectantly looking to You, Lord.
I will never give up hope as I wait on Your reply. I give my
life and all that I love into Your hands, knowing that You
have only the best in mind for me. For You are a loving
Father who delights in a faithful daughter. I thank You, Lord,
for all that You have done, are doing, and will do in my life!

Believe and Trust

Let us then fearlessly and confidently and boldly draw near to the throne of grace (the throne of God's unmerited favor to us sinners), that we may receive mercy [for our failures] and find grace to help in good time for every need [appropriate help and well-timed help, coming just when we need it].
HEBREWS 4:16 AMP

An amazing confidence is available to the woman who seeks God's face, believes in His Word, and trusts in the power of His grace. It gives us the same intense energy that strengthened the apostles and enabled Stephen to work great miracles among God's people.

Yet there is a paradox. For it is through our weakness that Christ's strength and power is made perfect—all enabling! Think of it! Knowing we are perfectly and abundantly empowered by God, we need not be afraid of anything as we confidently rest in Christ and live in God's love! The power of God's grace will come at the exact moment and enable us to do whatever is necessary. The seemingly impossible is now possible. This is what separates the Christians from the rest of the crowd!

Acts 20:32 says that the "Word of His grace" not only builds us up but gives us an "inheritance among all God's set-apart ones (those consecrated, purified, and transformed of soul)" (AMP). And set apart we are! We don't need to find strength and confidence outside ourselves but merely tap into Christ's transforming power from within. What an incredible lift for the woman who stands not on her own, but on God, His Word, and His grace!

Casting Cares

The Lord said to her, "My dear Martha, you are worried and upset over all these details! There is only one thing worth being concerned about. Mary has discovered it, and it will not be taken away from her."
LUKE 10:41–42 NLT

All the "what if" supposing in life can leave a person bereft of peace. For that worrywart's focus is no longer on the Word and frame of one called Jesus Christ but is on the myriad of possibilities that may never actually happen. What a waste of God-given energy for the distracted diva whose song of trust, triumph, and tranquility is being drowned out by worldly woes.

Better that we be like Mary who sought and was concerned about only one thing—dwelling in God's Word, beholding His beauty, and meditating in His temple (see Psalm 27:4). When we're in His presence, no evil, no worry, no "what ifs" can reach us. He is a strong tower, a refuge, a depository for our cares.

Caretaker is defined as "a person who takes care of a vulnerable person, often a close relative." It is a wise woman who accepts Jesus Christ as the taker of her cares. She knows that when she commits herself—mind, body, spirit, soul, and heart—and her life to the Lord, she is in the best of places, reposing at His feet, listening to His voice, praising His name, and simply resting, trusting He will see her through every situation. Blessed is the woman who allows Christ to be her Caretaker—in this life and the next.

"Blessed is the man who trusts in the LORD,
And whose hope is the LORD.
For he shall be like a tree planted by the waters,
Which spreads out its roots by the river,
And will not fear when heat comes;
But its leaf will be green,
And will not be anxious in the year of drought,
Nor will cease from yielding fruit."
JEREMIAH 17:7–8 NKJV

Our lives are full of supposes. Suppose this should happen,
or suppose that should happen; what could we do;
how could we bear it? But, if we are living in the high tower
of the dwelling place of God, all these supposes will drop
out of our lives. We shall be quiet from the fear of evil, for no
threatenings of evil can penetrate into the high tower of God.
HANNAH WHITALL SMITH

How awesome to know, Lord, that from the day of my birth
You have been caring for me. And that You will continue to
do so throughout my life. Because You will always be here
for me, I need not worry about anything. Help me, Lord,
to keep that thought in the forefront of my mind. Help me
to realize that the concerns I have for today are
only passing, but You are forever.

Consolation Shared

I waited patiently and expectantly for the Lord; and He inclined to me and heard my cry. He drew me up out of a horrible pit. . . . He has put a new song in my mouth, a song of praise to our God. Many shall see and fear (revere and worship) and put their trust and confident reliance in the Lord.
PSALM 40:1—3 AMP

When God created woman, He made her a passionate, nurturing, caring being. Because of this, we women are guilty of carrying the weight of others, especially loved ones, upon our own small shoulders. Fortunately God, keenly aware of this, provided us with a way to help lift that burden—the gift of prayer.

When we meet the Creator in prayer, the weights we carry are lifted off our shoulders. In blessed spiritual communion with the Lord, we find that faith, hope, love, and joy cannot help but increase. We're compelled to sing songs of celebration, thanking and praising God for all He has done, is doing, and will do for us and our loved ones. An overwhelming peace springs up because prayer reminds us that our current circumstances will soon be over. One day, we will be called homeward to live with our Father forever in mansions of glory. But for now, we are comforted knowing prayer is the bridge between this world and the next, and will forever be a privilege and spirit booster to everyone who wholeheartedly relies on her Creator.

Lofty Height

*Looking away [from all that will distract] to Jesus, Who is the Leader
and the Source of our faith [giving the first incentive for our belief] and is
also its Finisher [bringing it to maturity and perfection]. He, for the joy
[of obtaining the prize] that was set before Him, endured the cross. . .
and is now seated at the right hand of the throne of God.*
HEBREWS 12:2 AMP

Moses brought God's children to the borders of Canaan, went atop
Mount Pisgah to view the Promised Land, and then died on that
lofty height (see Deuteronomy 34). Commenting on this story,
Matthew Henry wrote that God's law brings His people "into the
wilderness of conviction, but not into the Canaan of rest and settled
peace." That "spiritual rest of conscience and the eternal rest in
heaven" can only be accessed through Jesus.

The Promised Land is not an actual *place* but the *person* of Christ,
the reward received when we accept Him as Lord of our lives and then
abide in Him—here on earth and someday in heaven. To reach that
Promised Land, we can't allow earthly things and people to distract
us, but look wholeheartedly to Jesus to lead us through the wilderness.
Focused on Christ, we'll have all the manna and living water we need
for the journey. No longer preoccupied with or drawn away by the
trappings of this world, we'll ascend to a lofty height to view our true
home. There, abiding in the love and light of Christ, we'll reach the
peace of the Promised Land.

Seizing the Prize

And after my skin, even this body, has been destroyed, then from my flesh
or without it I shall see God, Whom I, even I, shall see for myself and
on my side! And my eyes shall behold Him, and not as a stranger!
JOB 19:26–27 AMP

While on this side of heaven, we can reach the Promised Land by
prayer in communion with Christ. But someday prayer will fall away
as God calls us, His daughters, home.

Once in His mansion, our earthly bodies will be perfected, and
we'll reach the haven where Christ, God, angels, and all the saints who
have gone before reside! In eternal life we will see and talk with God
and His Son face to face. In this ethereal place, filled with love and
light, all will be made known.

For once, there will be no niggling thoughts about our
imperfections. Impatience will fade away. Sorrow will disappear,
problems dissipate. There will be no barrier between us and our
heavenly Father and His Son.

And then one final day, when Christ unites the entire world with
God, we will see the new heaven and the new earth, a place free from
everything evil. There we will bask in the light the Lord God shines
on His city.

But until those days, we may praise God that our passage to the
Promised Land remains clear through the avenue of the sweet hour of
prayer.

The Spirit of God, who raised Jesus from the dead, lives in you. And just as God raised Christ Jesus from the dead, he will give life to your mortal bodies by this same Spirit living within you.
ROMANS 8:11 NLT

Ye do well to remember that habitual affectionate communion with God, asking Him for all good which is needed, praising Him for all that is received, and trusting Him for future supplies, prevents anxious cares; inspires peace, calmness, and composure; and furnishes a delight surpassing all finite comprehension.
JAMES H. AUGHEY

I am here before You, Lord, longing to be dissolved in You. I long for the day when there will be no more pain or sorrow. When You will be upon the throne, reigning over a new heaven and earth. You have given me eternal life, Lord. Help me to make my years here count until I meet You down by the River of Life.

Count Your Blessings

When upon life's billows you are tempest-tossed,
When you are discouraged, thinking all is lost,
Count your many blessings, name them one by one,
And it will surprise you what the Lord hath done.

Chorus
Count your blessings, name them one by one,
Count your blessings, see what God hath done!
Count your blessings, name them one by one,
Count your many blessings, see what God hath done.

Are you ever burdened with a load of care?
Does the cross seem heavy you are called to bear?
Count your many blessings, every doubt will fly,
And you will keep singing as the days go by.

When you look at others with their lands and gold,
Think that Christ has promised you His wealth untold;
Count your many blessings—wealth can never buy
Your reward in heaven, nor your home on high.

So, amid the conflict whether great or small,
Do not be discouraged, God is over all;
Count your many blessings, angels will attend,
Help and comfort give you to your journey's end.
JOHNSON OATMAN JR., 1897

Johnson Oatman Jr. was a bivocational Methodist minister in New Jersey in the late 1800s. Having grown up in a godly home where hymns were frequently sung, he drew on that rich heritage as an adult and penned over five thousand hymns of his own. "Count Your Blessings" has been considered by many to be his finest. One writer described it this way: "It is like a beam of sunlight that has brightened up the dark places of the earth." It was so popular in Great Britain at one point that it was said, "The men sing it, the boys whistle it, and the women rock their babies to sleep on this hymn."

During the Welsh Revival of the early 1900s it was sung at every service, and for over a century it has been a popular song to sing on Thanksgiving Day.

Name Them One by One

Return to your rest, my soul, for the LORD has been
good to you. For you, LORD, have delivered me from
death, my eyes from tears, my feet from stumbling.
PSALM 116:7 NIV

Counting our blessings can transform our outlook on life. When life
is overwhelming and out of control, we can rest. We can trust the
God who has been faithful in the past, to be faithful now and in all
the days to come. God has blessed us abundantly! He has rescued us
from death, from despair, and from humiliation. Sit down and count
all of the ways that God has blessed you. Don't just go over them in
your mind, take the time to write them down! Then when you are
tempted to stress over life issues again (and those days are sure to
come), you can look back at your list of blessings and remember all
the ways that God has been faithful to you. The Bible tells us that
God is the same yesterday, today, and forever (Hebrews 13:8). Relax
in that truth and allow God to transform your mind-set into one of
thankfulness, blessing, and peace.

Finding Encouragement

"This is my command—be strong and courageous!
Do not be afraid or discouraged.
For the LORD your God is with you wherever you go."
JOSHUA 1:9 NLT

Discouragement is everywhere. Every step in the right direction is
often criticized by others. Friends, family, and even well-meaning
Christians can lose sight of faith and discourage us from following
God's will to the fullest. It's so important to keep our eyes on Christ
and concern ourselves only with what He wants for us and not what
others think. Find encouragement in the One who made you and
has perfect plans for your life. Going against the norm takes courage!
And God promises to be with you at all times. He is your constant
encourager and comforter. Allow Him to be the center of your life. . .
and His peace will guard your heart and mind (Philippians 4:6–7).
Now *that's* encouraging!

*Do not be anxious about anything, but in every situation,
by prayer and petition, with thanksgiving, present your requests
to God. And the peace of God, which transcends all understanding,
will guard your hearts and your minds in Christ Jesus.*
PHILIPPIANS 4:6–7 NIV

I find that doing of the will of God leaves
me no time for disputing about His plans.
GEORGE MACDONALD

Jesus, you are my friend, my comfort, and my constant
encourager. Help me to seek you always and not worry
about what others think. Your plan for my life is
perfect and full of promise. Amen.

Blessings in Burdens

All praise to God, the Father of our Lord Jesus Christ. God is our merciful Father and the source of all comfort. He comforts us in all our troubles so that we can comfort others. When they are troubled, we will be able to give them the same comfort God has given us. For the more we suffer for Christ, the more God will shower us with his comfort through Christ.

2 CORINTHIANS 1:3–5 NLT

Are you enrolled in the School of Hard Knocks? It may feel like that at times. The Bible tells us to expect trouble (John 16:33) because we live in a broken, fallen world. Knowing hard times are coming doesn't make it much easier, but Jesus offers us His peace at all times. We mistakenly believe that peace equals carefree days and tranquility. Missionary and author J. Oswald Sanders once said that peace isn't the absence of trouble, but the presence of God in the midst of trouble. The blessing of true peace gives us the ability to make it through anything knowing that God sees our progress report and is using every problem to teach us. And in turn, we can be a blessing by comforting and teaching others so that one day we will graduate with flying colors.

Simple Joys

The blessing of the LORD makes a person rich,
and he adds no sorrow with it.
PROVERBS 10:22 NLT

God's blessings—both large and small—do indeed make life rich. Instead of asking "What's next, God?" make time to thank Him for what He's already given you. Instead of asking "Why not me, God?" delight with your friends and family who are being blessed. Look around you and see the simple joys that God has added to your world. Take joy in the children in your life, their simple faith and absolute trust in God. Enjoy God's creation all around you, the beauty in each season. Invest in the people God has placed on your path, the joy of loving and being loved. It is in these simple joys that the stuff of life is made full and we see God's blessings in everyday life. Don't take any of them for granted! As Walter Hagen, the American golfer once said: "You're only here for a short visit. Don't hurry, don't worry. And be sure to smell the flowers along the way."

For you make me glad by your deeds, LORD;
I sing for joy at what your hands have done.
PSALM 92:4 NIV

Blessed be Your name
On the road marked with suffering
Though there's pain in the offering
Blessed be Your name
MATT REDMAN

Heavenly Father, thank You for the simple joys of life:
my health, my family, my friends. Help me to slow down
and appreciate all the blessings in my life. You have provided
me with everything I need and have blessed me abundantly.
Help me delight in the little gifts You bring
my way every day. Amen.

A Song in My Heart

I will give thanks to you, LORD, with all my heart;
I will tell of all your wonderful deeds.
I will be glad and rejoice in you;
I will sing the praises of your name, O Most High.
PSALM 9:1—2 NIV

If we are daily praising God and our hearts are full of love for Him, others cannot help but see the difference He has made in our lives. Praise and worship isn't just about singing songs at church on Sunday. It's about living my life in such a way that is pleasing to God. If we are living a life of worship, we cannot help but tell others about who He is and what He has done for us. Do you have a song in your heart? Are you filled with joy over what God has done for us? If not, then confess your lack of contentment to the Lord and ask Him to fill you to overflowing with His love and joy. Put a smile on your face and focus on how much God loves you. Living with a song in your heart will make the Father smile and can be a great witness to others wherever you go.

Love: The Greatest Blessing

For God so loved the world that he gave his one and only Son, that whoever believes in him shall not perish but have eternal life. For God did not send his Son into the world to condemn the world, but to save the world through him.
JOHN 3:16–17 NIV

Do you know Jesus Christ as your personal Savior? If not, you are missing out on life. Everlasting life! Won't you take a moment right now and surrender your life to Him? We've all made mistakes, but the Bible tells us that God longs to be gracious and compassionate (Isaiah 30:18) and that if we accept His gift of salvation, we can be with Him for all eternity (Romans 6:23). God loved us all so much that He gave His son to take away our sins. The gift of salvation is just that: a gift. It is nothing you could ever earn. The love of God is the greatest of all gifts; the greatest of all blessings.

All praise to God, the Father of our Lord Jesus Christ,
who has blessed us with every spiritual blessing in the heavenly
realms because we are united with Christ. Even before he made
the world, God loved us and chose us in Christ to be
holy and without fault in his eyes.
EPHESIANS 1:3–4 NLT

Blue skies with white clouds on summer days. A myriad
of stars on clear moonlit nights. Tulips and roses and violets
and dandelions and daisies. Bluebirds and laughter and
sunshine and Easter. See how He loves us!
ALICE CHAPIN

What amazing love You have blessed us with, Father! A love
I do not deserve. Let my heart be filled with love for You so
that I can share this great blessing with others. You are my
hope in an often hopeless world. You are my hope of heaven;
my hope of peace; my hope of change, purpose,
and unconditional love. Amen.

He Keeps His Promises

*The LORD himself goes before you and will be with you; he will
never leave you nor forsake you. Do not be afraid; do not be discouraged.*
DEUTERONOMY 31:8 NIV

Multiple times throughout the Bible, God promises that He will
never leave us nor forsake us. Christians throughout the ages will
testify that God keeps His promises and that He is always with
us. Even when it feels that we are far from God or that He doesn't
see our circumstances, He is never far from any of us (Acts 17:27).
When your faith is small and you have trouble trusting that God will
do what He promised, look back on all of the blessings that you've
claimed in your lifetime and ask the Lord to remind you of His
faithfulness. He keeps His promises. When no one else in your life is
worthy of your trust, you have a heavenly Father who can be counted
on to do what He said He will do. People will let you down. Jesus
never will. People will break promises. Jesus never will. The Lord is
always with you and you can trust Him!

Simple, Everyday Blessings

*Since, then, you have been raised with Christ, set your hearts on
things above, where Christ is seated at the right hand of God.
Set your minds on things above, not on earthly things.*
COLOSSIANS 3:1—2 NIV

We are often bombarded with troubles in this life: health issues,
financial crises, relationship problems, and many other daily trials
that break our spirits. Jesus beckons us to focus on Him instead of
worldly worries. Just as Peter walked on the water until he took his
eyes off Christ and looked at the impossible mess he was in, so will
we miss out on many of life's simple blessings when we look around
at our own problems instead of setting our gaze on the Lord. God
wants to bless us in the midst of the mess of life. Daily He sends
little reminders that He is with us and watching over us. Take a look
around you and thank God for all of the simple blessings that we
often take for granted. If our hearts are set on things above, we'll
never miss the simple, everyday blessings that God sends our way.

How joyful are those who fear the LORD—
all who follow his ways!
You will enjoy the fruit of your labor.
How joyful and prosperous you will be!
PSALM 128:1–2 NLT

The heart is rich when it is content, and it is
always content when its desires are fixed on God.
MIGUEL FEBRES CORDERO-MUÑOZ

When I set my mind on You, heavenly Father, I'm much
more aware of the simple and many ways You bless me
every day. Be the center of my day so that I don't miss
out on what You want to show me. I don't want to dwell
on what might happen in the future; I want to relish this
chance to nurture and cherish the blessings
You've given me. Amen.

An Eternal Reward

For I am convinced that neither death nor life, neither angels nor demons, neither the present nor the future, nor any powers, neither height nor depth, nor anything else in all creation, will be able to separate us from the love of God that is in Christ Jesus our Lord.
ROMANS 8:38–39 NIV

God's Word tells us that He has set eternity in our hearts (Ecclesiastes 3:11). It is something that we long for all the days of our earthly life. God went to great lengths to make sure we could inherit His blessing of love and eternal life. He sent His Son, Jesus, to exhibit His love and make a way for us to be with Him for all eternity. He reminds us that nothing—absolutely nothing—can separate us from His love. That's our eternal reward—to live un-separated from God's love for all eternity! And we don't have to wait until heaven to receive *that* blessing. He offers His love to us right now. We just need to accept it and live in it as we look forward to eternity. Are you living in God's love? Ask the Lord to show you the truth of His love today. The rewards are eternal.

Blessed Freedom in Christ

It is for freedom that Christ has set us free. Stand firm, then,
and do not let yourselves be burdened again by a yoke of slavery.
GALATIANS 5:1 NIV

Freedom in Christ is more than just being free from sin and securing
our place in heaven. Freedom in Christ means that we can be free
here and now—to live a life of purpose, to hope and to dream. We
don't have to be imprisoned by negative thinking or worried about
what others think of us. We don't have to watch our backs or concern
ourselves over idle gossip. Freedom in Christ gives us confidence
to be all that God made us to be. We are no longer held captive
by fear! The perfect love that Christ offers us casts out all fear (1
John 4:18), and we can have true peace—a peace that transcends all
understanding—here on earth while we live our daily lives. When we
live like we're free in Christ, our insecurities fade, our fears diminish,
and love takes over.

*"Only in returning to me
and resting in me will you be saved.
In quietness and confidence is your strength."*
ISAIAH 30:15 NLT

Those who run in the path of God's
commands have their hearts set free.
JOANIE GARBORG

Father, thank You for the freedom You've given me
in Christ! Freedom to live for You, to dream, to hope,
and to live a life of meaning. You have freed me from death.
You have freed me from my enemies. I praise You and
worship You for all You have done! Amen.

He's in Control

> *"The God who made the world and everything in it is the Lord
> of heaven and earth and does not live in temples built by human hands.
> And he is not served by human hands, as if he needed anything.
> Rather, he himself gives everyone life and breath and everything else."*
> ACTS 17:24–25 NIV

Isn't it amazing that the God who formed the earth and established it upon the waters is the same God who knows us intimately and wants a very personal relationship with us? God's Word tells us that He knows when we sit down and stand up. He knows our words before we speak them! (Psalm 139). God had already determined where and when we should live long before we were ever born. What a comfort to know He's in control! He knows everything that has happened and will happen to us. He is not far from any of us! Everything that comes our way has passed through His hands first. We are safe in His arms.

Comfort for Today

I remain confident of this:
I will see the goodness of the LORD
in the land of the living.
Wait for the LORD;
be strong and take heart
and wait for the LORD.
PSALM 27:13–14 NIV

God never changes. He sees His people through hard times. God is good, and He is working everything that happens in your life for *your* good (Romans 8:28). Be comforted today knowing if we wait on the Lord and trust in His purpose and timing, we will see His goodness in this life. If we cast our burdens and cares on Him, He will sustain us and won't let us fall (Psalm 55:22). Know that God sees your situation and your circumstances. He loves you and He cares. Trust that He is working in your life, behind the scenes, orchestrating a grand finale that you can't hear or see just yet. Ask for His guidance and seek His face today as you wait on Him. And be on the lookout for the miracles and blessings—big and small—that God is sending your way.

"The LORD will guide you always;
he will satisfy your needs in a sun-scorched land
and will strengthen your frame.
You will be like a well-watered garden,
like a spring whose waters never fail."
ISAIAH 58:11 NIV

Let the matchless love of God sweep away
your doubts and fears. You already have
God's attention, and you will never lose it.
JONI EARECKSON TADA

Father God, how amazing it is to me that You are the
creator of the universe—You're the one who placed
the stars in the sky—and yet You care for me deeply!
When I put my life in Your hands, I am safe. Amen.

Cultivating a Thankful Heart

I will praise you, LORD, with all my heart;
before the "gods" I will sing your praise.
I will bow down toward your holy temple
and will praise your name
for your unfailing love and your faithfulness,
for you have so exalted your solemn decree
that it surpasses your fame.
PSALM 138:1–2 NIV

Start your morning by thanking God for a new day, knowing that His mercies and compassion are new every morning (Lamentations 3:22–23). Keep a song of praise in your heart throughout the day, thanking God for His many blessings. Thank Him for the simple things in life: meals, friends, family, smiles from children, a roof over your head, a warm place to sleep, clothing, and transportation. Say "Thank You!" *out loud* to God. Tell Him how thankful you are for His love, for His son, for His gift of life now and for eternity. In the evening, thank Him for family time, for a job that provides, for a freshly prepared dinner. As you rest your head on your pillow, thank God for a full day, for the little blessings you witnessed throughout the day, for how He was with you through it all, and will be again tomorrow and for all eternity. *That's* how you cultivate a thankful heart.

Being a Blessing to Others

"Give, and it will be given to you. A good measure, pressed down,
shaken together and running over, will be poured into your lap.
For with the measure you use, it will be measured to you."
LUKE 6:38 NIV

When we give of ourselves without seeking our own glory, God will
bless that abundantly! There is so much joy in forgetting yourself
and knowing that someone else is being blessed by what you've done.
Sometimes our good deeds go unnoticed by people, but don't let this
stop you. Let others see Christ shining through you! Ask God to
show you how you might bless another person *without* getting noticed
today. If we're doing everything for the glory of God, it won't matter
if others take notice or not. But if they do notice our good deeds,
our hope is that they will praise God and see His love through what
you've done. And don't forget to give back to God what He's given
you by tithing. He promises to bless you when you do so (Malachi
3:10). If all Christians gave back their tithe as God has asked, there
would be enough food and supplies for everyone in need.

And It Will Surprise You
What the Lord Has Done

But let all who take refuge in you be glad;
let them ever sing for joy.
Spread your protection over them,
that those who love your name may rejoice in you.
Surely, LORD, you bless the righteous;
you surround them with your favor as with a shield.
PSALM 5:11—12 NIV

Have you sat down and counted your blessings? Have you written them down? It's so important to journal God's miracles and blessings in your life so that you can see all that the Lord has done for you. Take the time to count and record your blessings. Write them in a journal, start a blog, create a blessing scrapbook—whatever works best for you. And keep it handy! Remember that hard times will come your way. That's a guarantee in this old world. But won't it be great to pull out your chronicle of God's blessings in your own life in the midst of your trials? Not only will that help you get your mind off of your temporary troubles, you can worship and praise God as you recount the ways He has been faithful to you in the past. What a blessing!

"Bring all the tithes into the storehouse so there will be enough food in my Temple. If you do," says the LORD of Heaven's Armies, "I will open the windows of heaven for you. I will pour out a blessing so great you won't have enough room to take it in! Try it! Put me to the test!"
MALACHI 3:10 NLT

We are to turn our back upon evil, and in every way possible, do good, help people, and bring blessings into their lives.
NORMAN VINCENT PEALE

Father God, though Your strength is limitless, it's tempered with wisdom and gentleness. You are both my strong tower and my tender, loving Father. You have given me everything! You have blessed me beyond my imagination and have called me Your child.

Great Is Thy Faithfulness

Great is Thy faithfulness, O God my Father;
There is no shadow of turning with Thee;
Thou changest not, Thy compassions, they fail not.
As Thou hast been, Thou forever wilt be.

Refrain
Great is Thy faithfulness!
Great is Thy faithfulness!
Morning by morning new mercies I see.
All I have needed Thy hand hath provided;
Great is Thy faithfulness, Lord, unto me!

Summer and winter and springtime and harvest,
Sun, moon, and stars in their courses above
Join with all nature in manifold witness
To Thy great faithfulness, mercy, and love.

Pardon for sin and a peace that endureth
Thine own dear presence to cheer and to guide;
Strength for today and bright hope for tomorrow,
Blessings all mine, with ten thousand beside!
THOMAS O. CHISHOLM, 1923

Thomas Chisholm was plagued by poor health throughout his life. At times, his health was so fragile he was unable to work. One of his favorite scripture passages was Lamentations 3:22–23: "Through the LORD's mercies we are not consumed, because His compassions fail not. They are new every morning; great is Your faithfulness" (NKJV). Out of a heart full of gratitude for the Lord's faithfulness in his weakness, he penned the words to "Great Is Thy Faithfulness" and sent them to his musician friend William Runyan. Runyan was so moved by the words he composed the tune to accompany it. The hymn was first published in 1923, but its popularity skyrocketed when it was discovered by George Beverly Shea and sung at Billy Graham crusades around the world.

God's Great Faithfulness

Thy mercy, O LORD, is in the heavens;
and thy faithfulness reacheth unto the clouds.
PSALM 36:5 KJV

"Great Is Thy Faithfulness" is a beautiful, beloved hymn, and it is even more beautiful when we look deeper into its meaning. The dictionary gives one meaning of *faithfulness* as "loyalty." In a fallen world, people unfortunately often fail at loyalty. Marriages fall apart; families feud among themselves; deep and lasting friendships are hard to come by. Since we humans mess it up so much, many people often think of a beloved pet dog—man's best friend—as the image of ultimate loyalty. But the God who said "I will never leave you nor forsake you" (Hebrews 13:5 ESV) is the only One truly unfaltering and untiring in His loyalty to His people.

Faithfulness is also defined as a "firm keeping of promises." We've all experienced the disappointment from a promise not kept. And no matter how good and strong our intentions, we're all guilty of breaking promises to others, too. God, however, will never let us down with a broken promise. Deuteronomy 7:9 tells us, "Understand, therefore, that the LORD your God is indeed God. He is the faithful God who keeps his covenant for a thousand generations and lavishes his unfailing love on those who love him and obey his commands" (NLT).

Finally *faithfulness* is "worthiness of trust." Who is worthier of our trust than the God who created every detail about us (Psalm 139:13), has every hair on our heads numbered (Matthew 10:30), has good plans for us and our futures (Jeremiah 29:11), and who gave up His own Son to die that we might live (John 3:16–17)? God abundantly fulfills every meaning of the word *faithful.* Yes, "*great* is Thy faithfulness"!

Faithful Father

*See what great love the Father has lavished on us, that we
should be called children of God! And that is what we are!*
1 JOHN 3:1 NIV

Life is impossible without a father, but not everyone has or knows
their earthly father or ever had a good one. For those who have or
had a good one, the word *father* might equate with things like big,
warm bear hugs and a sense of strength and security. For those who
don't or didn't, the word *father* might evoke sadness, bitterness, and
tears—tragically, even fear. For those blessed with a good earthly
father, the connection to our heavenly Father is often not difficult.
When the Bible talks about God being our *Abba* (a Hebrew word
that is a more intimate word for *father*, like *daddy*), those people can
quickly relate and think of God as Provider, Comforter, Teacher,
and Friend. But for those who have never experienced a healthy and
loving paternal relationship, they have a choice: either build a wall of
rejection or unbelief against God our heavenly Father, likening Him
to their sinful human father, or reach out to Abba and fall into His
divine arms, letting His perfect love and faithfulness soothe their
hurt and fulfill their needs. Whether good or bad, no earthly father is
perfect. Even the best are simply human and will fail us at times. But
our God, to whom we can sing, "Great is Thy faithfulness, O God
my Father," is absolutely perfect and absolutely faithful. His love and
His care will never, ever let us down.

*Those who know your name trust in you,
for you, LORD, have never forsaken those who seek you.*
PSALM 9:10 NIV

Trusting God completely means having faith that He
knows what is best for your life. You expect Him to
keep His promises, help you with problems, and do
the impossible when necessary.
RICK WARREN

Dear Father, I fail so often in my faithfulness to others and
to You. Like Jacob prayed in Genesis 32, I am not worthy of
even the least of all the things You have done for me in Your
steadfast love and constant faithfulness. Regardless, You
continue to love and bless and provide for me. I can't thank
You enough. Please forgive me for my lack of faithfulness
and help me to model Yours. Amen.

Faithfully Unchanging

God also bound himself with an oath, so that those who received the promise could be perfectly sure that he would never change his mind. So God has given both his promise and his oath. These two things are unchangeable because it is impossible for God to lie. Therefore, we who have fled to him for refuge can have great confidence as we hold to the hope that lies before us.
Hebrews 6:17–18 NLT

You only have to look at a baby's photos from month to month to see how quickly life can change. Unfortunately, not all changes are as sweet as those of a healthy baby's growth and development. Just read or listen to the news for plenty of examples. Many of life's changes are utterly devastating. And for some, even small changes cause major stress. For the most part, we like to settle deep down into our comfort zones with a satisfied *ahhhh* and pray for no disruptions. Unfortunately, the disruptions are inevitable. But in a world where it seems nothing much stays the same for more than a few minutes or months at most, isn't it good to know that there is an almighty God who is our one true constant? As the song goes, "There is no shadow of turning with Thee; Thou changest not. . ." These words are a reference to the King James Version of James 1:17, which says, "Every good gift and every perfect gift is from above, and cometh down from the Father of lights, with whom is no variableness, neither shadow of turning." An updated version reads, "Whatever is good and perfect comes down to us from God our Father, who created all the lights in the heavens. He never changes or casts a shifting shadow" (NLT).

The song and the scripture are making the point that God does not change. *Ever.* No matter how far out of our comfort zones change takes us, we can find lasting, permanent comfort in our unchanging heavenly Father.

Faithfully Compassionate

The LORD passed in front of Moses, calling out, "Yahweh!
The LORD! The God of compassion and mercy! I am slow
to anger and filled with unfailing love and faithfulness."
EXODUS 34:6 NLT

Henry Ward Beecher once said, "God pardons like a mother, who kisses the offense into everlasting forgiveness." Our God is our heavenly Father, but His compassion for us is perhaps best exhibited in the way He created mothers to care for and love their children. A good mother has endless, unconditional love and compassion for her children, and no amount of anger or mistakes will ever change that. Ask any mother who has held her arms open to a child with fat tears spilling from his sorrowful eyes, hiccupping out, "I'm sorry!" Or ask the mother who has helped hold down a child during a painful medical procedure or stood beside her child's hospital bed, praying desperately that she might take the pain herself instead.

As hard as it is to imagine, God's love and compassion for us is even better than a devoted mother. Like the song says, "Thy compassions they fail not"—they cannot fail because He *is* love. No matter what we do, no matter how angry and hurt our *sin* might make Him, He still loves *us*, His children. In Isaiah He asks, "Can a woman forget her nursing child, and not have compassion on the son of her womb? Surely they may forget, yet I will not forget you" (49:15 NKJV). A mother's compassions rarely fail; God's compassions *never* fail.

But you, Lord, are a compassionate and gracious God,
slow to anger, abounding in love and faithfulness.
PSALM 86:15 NIV

Remember that even Jesus' most scathing denunciation—
a blistering diatribe against the religious leaders of Jerusalem
in Matthew 23—ends with Christ weeping over Jerusalem.
Compassion colored everything He did.
JOHN MACARTHUR

Dear Father, I'm so grateful that Your compassion will never fail
me, even when I least deserve it. With my sin I make such a mess
sometimes, but no matter how ugly the sins, You never reject me.
Like a dear mother's arms, Your arms are also always open and
waiting for me, ready to comfort and reassure me that You'll
never stop loving me. I can't thank You enough. Amen.

Faithfully Amazing

For the LORD is good and his love endures forever;
his faithfulness continues through all generations.
PSALM 100:5 NIV

"As Thou hast been, Thou forever wilt be. . . ." As complex and
capable as our human brains might be, we can't possibly fully wrap
them around the fact that God is eternal. There was no starting point
of God. His Old Testament name is *Yahweh*, which is a Hebrew word
for "I am." He revealed Himself to Moses in the burning bush,
saying, " 'I AM WHO I AM.' And he said, 'Say this to the people of
Israel, I AM has sent me to you'" (Exodus 3:14 ESV). God simply *is!*
He always has been, and He has no end. Psalm 90:2 (ESV) describes
God this way: "Before the mountains were brought forth, or ever you
had formed the earth and the world, from everlasting to everlasting
you are God." Other attributes of God include His immutability,
meaning He never changes (Malachi 3:6). God is omnipresent; He
is everywhere all the time (Psalm 139:7—10). God is omniscient; He
knows everything (Psalm 33:13—15). God is omnipotent; He can do
anything and has unlimited power (Genesis 18:14; Jeremiah 32:17).

How can we *not* trust such an awesome God? There is great
power and comfort in knowing that the one, true God is bigger and
better than all of our human ways and understanding. Because of
His divine, supernatural attributes and abilities, He is the only One
worthy of our complete trust. He is the only One *capable* of being
perfectly faithful to us!

Faithfully Merciful

The steadfast love of the LORD never ceases;
his mercies never come to an end;
they are new every morning;
great is your faithfulness.
LAMENTATIONS 3:22—23 ESV

It's oh so easy to get stuck in a rut of a sinful attitude or behavior. Even the apostle Paul said, "I don't really understand myself, for I want to do what is right, but I don't do it. Instead, I do what I hate" (Romans 7:15 NLT). At the end of a long, rotten day full of our failures, sometimes the best we can do is cry out to God for help and try to muddle through until we make it to a new day. What is it about a night of rest and waking up to another sunrise that can help us forget the mistakes of yesterday and start over again feeling forgiven and fresh? Maybe it's the fact that scripture says God's mercies are new every morning (Lamentation 3:22—23). Aren't you grateful you can sing, "Morning by morning new mercies I see," and know that it's true? Think how awful life would be if we had a heavenly Father who held our sins over our heads or kept endless grudges or pinned guilt trips on us—how depressing and defeating that would be! But no, our loving Father faithfully offers us new mercy every single day, forgetting our faults immediately when we admit them and ask His forgiveness.

Mercy is often described as God not giving us the punishment we really deserve. We sure do mess things up sometimes, but we are incredibly blessed to have a loving Father who forgives, forgets, and faithfully grants us mercy.

*If we confess our sins, he is faithful and just and will
forgive us our sins and purify us from all unrighteousness.*
1 JOHN 1:9 NIV

We fail Him, but, blessed be His name, He has never failed us,
and He never will do so. We doubt Him, we mistrust His love
and His providence and His guidance; we "faint because of
the way"; we murmur because of the way; yet all the time He
is there blessing us and waiting to pour out upon us a blessing
so great that there shall not be room to receive it.
UNKNOWN

Dear Father, I get so frustrated with myself for doing what
I know is wrong or struggling with the same problem over
and over again. Thank You for loving me anyway. Where would
I be without Your endless mercy on me? Thank You that
every single time I ask for Your forgiveness, You remove the
sin from me as far as the east is from the west.
Thank You, Savior, *thank You!* Amen.

Faithful Provider

He provides food for those who fear him;
he remembers his covenant forever.
PSALM 111:5 NIV

Life certainly has its up and downs, times of plenty and times of not so much, but no matter our present circumstances, we can constantly sing, "All I have needed Thy hand hath provided." The God who knows when each sparrow falls considers His children worth far more than just the birds (Matthew 10:28–31), and He promises to love and provide for us. Jesus specifically told us not to worry about food or drink or clothes, for our heavenly Father knows that we need these things. We simply seek Him and His righteousness first, and all these things will be given to us as well (Matthew 6:25–34).

Unfortunately, our culture and our selfish nature make it hard to be content with having only our basic needs met. We want it all, and we want it now! But the closer we draw to God, the less we desire the things of this world—the things that moth and rust destroy—and the more we long for our heavenly, eternal home and the treasures there that moth and rust cannot destroy (Matthew 6:19–21).

There's a joke that you'll never see a U-Haul attached to a hearse, and its point is true! So we must choose to focus less on material items that we can't take to eternity and more on the things that do matter forever—our relationship with God, our relationships with others, and our good works that will store treasure for us in heaven, like loving, giving, serving, and sharing the Gospel (1 Timothy 6:17–19).

When we seek after God wholeheartedly, only then will we fully realize how true it is that *everything* we truly need, "Thy hand hath provided."

Faithful Timekeeper

*My frame was not hidden from you when I was made in the
secret place, when I was woven together in the depths of the earth.
Your eyes saw my unformed body; all the days ordained for me
were written in your book before one of them came to be.*
PSALM 139:15–16 NIV

"Summer and winter and springtime and harvest. . ." Singing about
the seasons reminds us of the passing of time, and the older we get,
the faster it flies. Just like the seasons of the year, there are seasons
of life—sometimes difficult like a frigid, dark winter, sometimes
pleasant like a not-too-hot summer. No season is perfect, but with
the right attitude, we can find joy in them all. We might dread the
signs of cooler weather coming and the endless leaf raking, but we can
choose to delight in the colors of fall. We might detest the rains and
mud of spring but can be grateful that they bring new life and growth.

There is bitter and sweet in every season of life, but we need
to learn to accept them all, confident that God controls everything.
Psalm 31:15 (NIV) says, "My times are in your hands."

Our heavenly Father is our faithful timekeeper. 99

Every moment, every day, every season, every year—they are
all kept and watched over by our Sovereign God. All our days and
moments have been recorded by Him, from even before we were born
(Psalm 139:16). None of us can possibly know exactly how much time
we'll have on this earth, but we can trust our God to keep track. We
can choose to live whatever length of life we're given to His glory,
seeking out the joy that is always there amid the pain, knowing our
faithful timekeeper loves us and has good plans for us—and, even
better, is preparing a timeless eternity for us.

So teach us to number our days
that we may get a heart of wisdom.
Psalm 90:12 ESV

If God can make a billion galaxies, can't he make good
out of our bad and sense out of our faltering lives?
Of course he can. He is God.
MAX LUCADO

Dear Father, in such an uncertain world, it's so comforting to
know that You are keeping time. Since long before Creation,
You've had a sovereign schedule in place. It's not my job to
know or understand it, but I can choose to believe it is best.
You sent Your Son to save us according to Your timing,
and You will send Him again at just the right time. You gave
me life according to Your timing, and You will take me to
eternity at just the right time. Meanwhile, help me to live my life
honoring You with each moment You've given me. Amen.

Faithful Creator

In the beginning God created the heaven and the earth.
GENESIS 1:1 KJV

We only have to glance out a window or step outside to find
tangible evidence of God's amazing faithfulness. As the song goes,
the "sun, moon, and stars in their courses above, join with all nature
in manifold witness, to Thy great faithfulness, mercy, and love."
A stirring scripture that beautifully describes God as our faithful
Creator is Isaiah 40:28–31 (NIV):

> *"Do you not know? Have you not heard?*
> *The LORD is the everlasting God, the Creator of the ends of the earth.*
> *He will not grow tired or weary,*
> *and his understanding no one can fathom.*
> *He gives strength to the weary and increases the power of the weak.*
> *Even youths grow tired and weary,*
> *and young men stumble and fall;*
> *but those who hope in the LORD will renew their strength.*
> *They will soar on wings like eagles;*
> *they will run and not grow weary,*
> *they will walk and not be faint."*

The God who simply spoke not only our world but the entire
universe into existence surely has the power to help us, hold us, heal
us, and have mercy on us through His Son, Jesus Christ. May God's
marvelous creation remind us that He is our constant hope and He is
constantly faithful.

Faithful Savior and Peace

Then the angel said to them, "Do not be afraid, for behold, I bring
you good tidings of great joy which will be to all people. For there is
born to you this day in the city of David a Savior, who is Christ
the Lord. And this will be the sign to you: You will find a
Babe wrapped in swaddling cloths, lying in a manger."
LUKE 2:10–12 NKJV

The "Romans Road" is a clever name for key scriptures in the book of
Romans that walk us through the plan of salvation in Jesus Christ. We
are all sinners and fall short of God's glory (3:23). However, although
we were sinners, God showed us He loved us anyway by sending His
Son to die for us (5:8). There is a steep price for our sin—*death*—but
God provided the gift of Jesus Christ to cover the payment (6:23).
We simply must confess with our mouths and believe in our hearts
that God raised Jesus from the dead, and He is our Savior (10:9–10).
It sounds so simple; unfortunately, it's often easier said than done.
When sin and pride have a stronghold in a person's life, it can be
nearly impossible to let go, be humble, believe, and let God save. And
there are powerful enemies working hard to keep people from salvation
in Jesus (Ephesians 6:12). But those enemies have nothing on God's
power; for *nothing* is impossible with Him (Luke 1:37), *nothing* can
separate us from His love (Romans 8:38–39), and *nothing* and *no one*
other than Jesus Christ can save us (John 14:6; Acts 4:12).

"Pardon for sin and a peace that endureth. . ." There is no
greater example of God's faithfulness to us than when He gave up
His own Son to provide forgiveness for our sins and to be our Savior
and our peace.

Fear not, for I am with you;
be not dismayed, for I am your God.
ISAIAH 41:10 ESV

Because God is with you all the time, no place is any
closer to God than the place where you are right now.
RICK WARREN

Dear Father, I don't know what I would do or where I would
be without You. I'm so thankful I never have to walk a single
road or go through any season of life alone. I need Your guidance
and presence so much. You are constantly with me and know my
every move and every thought. Knowing this, I want to please
You and draw closer to You in all that I do. Amen.

Faithful Companion

He tends his flock like a shepherd:
He gathers the lambs in his arms
and carries them close to his heart;
he gently leads those that have young.
ISAIAH 40:11 NIV

Corrie ten Boom, a hero of the Christian faith during Adolf Hitler's reign of terror, endured unspeakable horrors during her time in prison and Nazi concentration camps. Her story of survival and triumph is truly miraculous. Our almighty God could have rescued her immediately from her plight, but He did not. For some people that causes doubt and anger, but for Corrie it was a God-given opportunity to share the light of Jesus in the darkest of places. That doesn't mean it wasn't awful, but Corrie knew God was constantly near. In her famous book, *The Hiding Place*, she prays, "Dear Jesus, how foolish of me to have called for human help when You are here." Hopefully we will never have to experience anything like a Nazi concentration camp, but our lives also have their hardships, even horrors. In the midst of them, it's easy to let ourselves believe God has abandoned us. Despite how we *feel* about what we're trying to endure, we must *choose* to trust God's promises, just like Corrie ten Boom did. We must cling to His Word to sustain us. And He has said, "Never will I leave you; never will I forsake you" (Hebrews 13:5 NIV).

Though we cannot understand all His ways, God is always with us; He is our most faithful companion. We never need to feel alone, and we can gratefully sing to Him our praises for His "dear presence to cheer and to guide."

Faithful Encourager and Guide

May the God of endurance and encouragement grant you to live in such harmony with one another, in accord with Christ Jesus, that together you may with one voice glorify the God and Father of our Lord Jesus Christ.
ROMANS 15:5–6 ESV

God's Word tells us many times to encourage each other in our faith, and we must strive to do so daily (Hebrews 3:13). But too often we fail each other. Not one of us is perfect; we will let down others who need encouragement, and we will be let down, too. That shouldn't stop us from trying, however; and thankfully God is a faithful encourager (Romans 15:5) who *never* fails us. When we are discouraged, the simple act of reading His Word and meditating on His promises has dramatic power to lift us up out of the deepest despair.

His Word is also a lamp for our feet and a light for our path (Psalm 119:105). Through His Word, He is our faithful Guide on every road of life, whether it's smooth, broad, and easy—or rocky, narrow, and hard. In every season and every circumstance, we can count on God to go before us and show us the way.

But He won't force us to follow Him. We can choose to find our own way—or we can choose to ask directions from the sovereign, all-knowing God who created everything and loves us more than anything. Obviously the latter is the wiser. "Thine own dear presence to cheer and to guide. . ." Our God knows us; He is rooting for us; He knows the best way for us. How blessed we are to never have to go it alone!

*"I will strengthen you and help you.
I will hold you up with my victorious right hand."*
ISAIAH 41:10 NLT

We can be tired, weary, and emotionally distraught,
but after spending time alone with God, we find that
He injects into our bodies energy, power, and strength.
CHARLES STANLEY

Dear Father, my human strength is nothing compared to
Your great strength, and only when I delight in my weakness
will I truly realize how strong You are. But my pride doesn't
easily delight in weakness. I like to be able to do things on
my own. Please humble me and make me weak so that You
can be strong in me and I can give all the glory to You. Amen.

Faithful Strength

God is our refuge and strength,
a very present help in trouble.
PSALM 46:1 KJV

An Old Testament name synonymous with the word *strength* is Samson. He was an ancient times Mr. Incredible, able to do things like tear apart an attacking lion with his bare hands (Judges 14:4–6) and fight off an army of a thousand men with the jawbone of a donkey (Judges 15:15–17). But his strength was not without conditions, and its secret was in his long locks of hair; his parents had promised God before his birth that it would never be cut. But then he met a woman named Delilah. . . . While there are plenty of strong and physically fit people in the world, there are no modern-day Samsons or Mr. Incredibles, and even the strongest person cannot maintain strength forever. Our bodies age and deteriorate, for we are, in fact, merely human. Thankfully God's strength has no conditions or limits. It can be trusted completely. He alone is our faithful Strength. We can confidently say, "My flesh and my heart may fail, but God is the strength of my heart and my portion forever" (Psalm 73:26 NIV).

As the song goes, He provides "strength for today" physically, emotionally, and spiritually, to face any and every challenge we might come up against—and not just today but *every* day.

Faithful Hope

Why am I discouraged?
Why is my heart so sad? I will put my hope in God!
I will praise him again—my Savior and my God!
PSALM 42:5—6 NLT

Chuck Colson was an adviser to President Richard Nixon from 1969 to 1973, was deeply involved in the Watergate scandal, and was sentenced to federal prison for obstruction of justice. You'd think a man brought down from power like that would lose all hope—and he did lose hope in himself and in politics and in this world. But he found real and lasting hope in Jesus Christ. He became a Christian in 1973, and in 1974 he served seven months in prison. He was released with a new mission to start a prison ministry, which resulted in Prison Fellowship, the largest outreach to prisoners, ex-prisoners, and their families. Colson said once in a famous speech, "Where is the hope? I meet millions of people that tell me that they feel demoralized by the decay around us. Where is the hope? The hope that each of us has is not in who governs us, or what laws are passed, or what great things we have planned, it is God working through the hearts of people. That's where our hope lies in this country. And that's where our hope lies in our life." We are often part of the millions Colson refers to who feel demoralized by decay. And if we put our hope in anything other than God's power working through people, which He does through salvation in Jesus Christ, we will always end up defeated. He is our "bright hope for tomorrow," our faithful and lasting hope. Where is the hope, we ask? The answer is always in God our Father and our Savior Jesus Christ.

Faithfully Worthy

Make a joyful noise to the LORD, all the earth! Serve the LORD with gladness! Come into his presence with singing! Know that the LORD, he is God! It is he who made us, and we are his; we are his people, and the sheep of his pasture. Enter his gates with thanksgiving, and his courts with praise! Give thanks to him; bless his name! For the Lord is good; his steadfast love endures forever, and his faithfulness to all generations.

PSALM 100 ESV

"Great is Thy faithfulness, Great is Thy faithfulness. . .Great is Thy Faithfulness, Lord unto me." In the chorus of this beautiful hymn, we sing over and over of God's great faithfulness. He deserves our worship again and again—and again. He deserves it because He is always Sovereign, always Creator, always King of kings, always Lord of lords; yet He is also always our loving, everlasting Father whom we can call Abba and who never makes a mistake. He is faithfully unchanging, compassionate, amazing, and merciful. He faithfully provides for us and keeps time for us. He is our Savior, Encourager, and Guide. He is our faithful Strength, Hope, and Peace. For all of those reasons and many more, He is faithfully worthy of all our praise.

Revelation 4:8 (NLT) gives an extraordinary word picture of worship to God, describing living creatures who surround His throne day and night and who never stop singing these praises to Him: "Holy, holy, holy is the Lord God, the Almighty—the one who always was, who is, and who is still to come." As we go about the number of days we've been given, with our faithful God guiding and helping us, may we not only praise Him with song but strive to make our every thought and deed an act of worship to the only One who is *always* worthy.

*And so, dear brothers and sisters, I plead with you to give your
bodies to God because of all he has done for you. Let them be
a living and holy sacrifice—the kind he will find acceptable.
This is truly the way to worship him.*

ROMANS 12:1 NLT

The more you praise God, the more you become
God-conscious and absorbed in His greatness, wisdom,
faithfulness, and love. Praise reminds you of all that God
is able to do and of great things He has already done.

WESLEY L. DUEWEL

Father, forgive me that too often I'm just giving you lip
service and not wholehearted worship, like when I'm distracted
during the music at church and when I'm too flippant about
You and Your Word. I want to fully revere You for who You
are because You absolutely deserve it. I want You to be my all
in all. Help me to draw closer to You and worship You
with everything You've given me. Amen.

Wonderful Words of Life

Sing them over again to me,
Wonderful words of life,
Let me more of their beauty see,
Wonderful words of life;
Words of life and beauty
Teach me faith and duty.

Refrain
Beautiful words, wonderful words,
Wonderful words of life;
Beautiful words, wonderful words,
Wonderful words of life.

Christ, the blessed One, gives to all
Wonderful words of life;
Sinner, listen to the loving call,
Wonderful words of life;
All so freely given,
Wooing us to heaven.

Sweetly echo the Gospel call,
Wonderful words of life;
Offer pardon and peace to all,
Wonderful words of life;
Jesus, only Savior,
Sanctify us forever.
PHILIP P. BLISS, 1874

Philip P. Bliss was one of the most notable hymn writers of the late nineteenth century. Born in a log cabin in Pennsylvania, he was raised by godly parents who instilled in him a love for music. In his late teens he became a schoolmaster, but his real love was music. Taking classes and attending singing school, he pieced a musical education together. In 1857 he was discovered by William Bradbury, a noted composer of sacred music, who persuaded him to devote himself to the Lord's service. Eventually Bliss became a well-recognized music teacher, song leader, and hymn writer.

His life was tragically cut short at age thirty-eight in a fiery train crash, but not before he had written and composed some of the most beloved hymns of the Christian church, including "Hold the Fort," "Jesus Loves Even Me," and the music for Horatio Spafford's "It Is Well with My Soul," composed one month before his death.

Wonderful Words of Life

In the beginning was the Word, and the Word was with God, and the Word was God. . . . In Him was life, and the life was the Light of men.
JOHN 1:1, 4 NASB

Every day, Jesus encountered people who were oppressed, poor, and without hope. They were harassed and helpless, sheep without a shepherd (Matthew 9:36). Each word spoken by the Word offered life to their dry and weary souls. While He warned that Satan would try to kill, steal, and destroy that hope, He promised a rich and abundant life to all who would confess and believe on His name.

As promising as they were then and are today, Jesus' words are also ironic, because abundant life typically doesn't mean our circumstances will change. He doesn't always remove the hardship, the storms, the pain, or the oppression. He does, however, allow us to experience inexplicable peace in the midst of the storm, hope in the midst of pain, and mighty strength in the midst of helplessness. In the pages that follow are Jesus' wonderful words of life. Embrace them for all the life they have to offer you.

Words of Truth

"I am. . .the truth."
JOHN 14:6 NIV

The rich young ruler was wealthy. He didn't lie, cheat, or steal. He hadn't killed anyone. He honored his parents, was kind to his neighbors. He was still missing something, and he knew Jesus would have the answer. "What good thing must I do to get eternal life?" he asked (Matthew 19:16 NIV). In His usual no-nonsense fashion, Jesus delivered the truth: "If you want to be perfect, go, sell your possessions and give to the poor, and you will have treasure in heaven. Then come, follow me." This was a hard truth to swallow, especially for a rich man. He walked away. Others, like the disciples, dropped everything to follow Him. Some wept at His feet, others knew if they merely touched the hem of His garment, they would be forever changed.

Whether they were rich or poor, powerful or despised, everyone Jesus encountered had no choice but to respond to His truth. There was no middle ground. They either received it and acted on it, or rejected it and walked away. You have this same opportunity. How will you respond to His truth?

Listen carefully to my words.
Don't lose sight of them.
Let them penetrate deep into your heart,
for they bring life to those who find them,
and healing to their whole body.
PROVERBS 4:20–22 NLT

When I no more can stir my soul to move,
And life is but the ashes of a fire;
When I can but remember that my heart
Once used to live and love, long and aspire—
O be thou then the first, the one thou art;
Be thou the calling, before all answering love,
And in me wake hope, fear, boundless desire.
GEORGE MACDONALD

Jesus, I confess that I am distracted by many things
that interfere with my ability to live abundantly for You.
I pray that You would free me from the temptation to
lose myself in trivial matters. Instead, capture my attention
and draw it to You, and You alone. Amen.

Words of Beauty

Jesus replied, "Leave her alone. She did this in preparation for my burial. You will always have the poor among you, but you will not always have me."
JOHN 12:7–8 NLT

Perhaps Mary had been saving the jar of expensive perfume for a special occasion, maybe the wedding of a friend or a family celebration. But this night, as she prepared to dine with Jesus and His disciples, she knew the moment had arrived. In a simple act of beauty, she lovingly anointed Jesus' feet and wiped them with her hair. Is it possible she knew what was to come? Did she know His feet would soon walk the long road to Calvary, or that in a very short time, nails would pierce His precious flesh? Perhaps, but perhaps she was merely overwhelmed by love for her beloved friend, the one who wept when she wept. Not quite the stuff of beauty, washing feet, but devotion to her Lord made it all worthwhile. Judas, his eyes blinded by sin and ulterior motive, was incapable of seeing the beauty in this quiet moment. He missed it entirely. Only those of a pure heart and mind can see the beauty of the Lord.

Words of Faith

Jesus turned around, and when he saw her he said,
"Daughter, be encouraged! Your faith has made you well."
MATTHEW 9:22 NLT

She had exhausted her resources. She had visited doctor after doctor, desperate for a cure as the life drained out of her, her health worsening by the day. Then she heard about Jesus, a man they called the Healer. Somehow she knew if she could just touch Him—ever so briefly—she would be made well. When her childlike faith encountered the mighty touch of the Healer, the charge was electric. He felt the power leave Him and touch her to the core. Her life would never be the same. She was free.

Did this woman consider herself to possess great faith? Doubtful. It seems she reached out to Him more out of desperation than mountain-moving faith. However, Jesus promised that a mustard-seed speck is all that's required. Do you have even a mustard seed's worth of faith? Reach out with it, and touch Him. You will never be the same.

Charm is deceptive, and beauty does not last;
but a woman who fears the LORD will be greatly praised.
PROVERBS 31:30 NLT

The whole being of any Christian is faith and love.
Faith brings the man to God, love brings him to men.
MARTIN LUTHER

Father, in a world filled with visual images and man-made
trinkets, it is easy to lose sight of what true beauty is. Instead
of investing my time and money in cultivating my outward
beauty, which does not last, help me to pour my resources into
cultivating a gentle and quiet spirit, the qualities you desire
in a woman who loves You. Amen.

Words of Duty

*Jesus replied, "And you experts in the law, woe to you,
because you load people down with burdens they can hardly
carry, and you yourselves will not lift one finger to help them."*
LUKE 11:46 NIV

While many of those who encountered Jesus were healed, freed, and transformed, the Pharisees were merely infuriated. Every word Jesus spoke cut straight to their hearts, but rather than allowing His truths to change them, they plotted to kill Him. Jesus and the Pharisees most often butted heads over the law. What was originally established to point the way to Christ had been reworked and adulterated, turned into a list of dos and don'ts that even the most righteous could never begin to uphold.

Although the Christian life is one of duty, Jesus challenged the Pharisees because they had "neglected the more important matters of the law—justice, mercy and faithfulness" (Matthew 23:23 NIV). They were so swallowed up in the details that the entire point had been long lost. Instead, Jesus asks that our duty flow out of grateful hearts that long to please Him.

Words of Blessing

Then Jesus called for the children and said to the disciples,
"Let the children come to me. Don't stop them! For the
Kingdom of God belongs to those who are like these children."
LUKE 18:16 NLT

The Sunday school version is idyllic. The dewy faced children sit at Jesus' feet, quietly gazing up at Him, waiting to hear what He will say. In reality, they were probably running and playing, interrupting grown-up conversations with their runny noses and dirt-smudged knees. The disciples were annoyed by their presence, scolding the parents for having such unruly children. Jesus saw them differently— interrupting their play for a moment, inviting them to come near. They skidded to a stop, surprised this gentle stranger might have something to say to them. And then He blessed them—gave them God's kingdom. The disciples must have been shocked that Jesus gave such a high place of honor to these bedraggled children.

Skid to a stop and turn to your Savior, right now, just as you are. He longs to lavish His blessing upon you.

"God blesses those who are humble,
for they will inherit the whole earth.
God blesses those who hunger and thirst for justice,
for they will be satisfied.
God blesses those who are merciful,
for they will be shown mercy.
God blesses those whose hearts are pure,
for they will see God.
God blesses those who work for peace,
for they will be called the children of God."
MATTHEW 5:5—9 NLT

It is not how much we have, but how
much we enjoy, that makes happiness.
CHARLES SPURGEON

Abba Father, Daddy. What a joy it is to be Your child.
How freeing it is to know that I don't have to clean myself
up to come before You. That You want me just as I am—
not the scrubbed-up Sunday school version of me, but the
Saturday-morning-playing-in-the-mud one who doesn't
quite have it all together. May nothing hinder me from
running straight into Your arms. Amen.

Words of Pardon

"Then neither do I condemn you," Jesus declared.
"Go now and leave your life of sin."
JOHN 8:11 NIV

The humiliation must have been unbearable. As if the scorning and judgmental faces of the townspeople weren't enough, the disdain from those who loved the woman caught in adultery would have made her crimson with shame. Would her family still claim her? Would her friends utter her name?

Everyone has a story, and no doubt the woman caught in adultery had hers. She had her reasons, more likely an act of desperation than wanton sin and debauchery. Perhaps it paid the bills, provided for her children, gave her a sense of power, or provided her with some sort of identity. Whatever the reason, being dragged through town and before Jesus no doubt caused her to reconsider. Surely she expected nothing but condemnation from this mysterious man who quietly wrote in the dirt. Instead, she received a gift. The gift of pardon. Sweet relief. What an unexpected, but cherished blessing.

No matter *what* you've done, this gift is yours for the taking.

Words of Promise

"For he made this promise to our ancestors,
to Abraham and his children forever."
LUKE 1:55 NLT

Can you imagine trying to grasp the news? Not only are you pregnant—a teenager no less—but you are also unmarried, a virgin. As if that isn't shocking enough, you happen to be carrying the promised Messiah in your womb. How could this possibly be so?

The first person Jesus touched on earth was His mother. Before He could even speak, the Word changed Mary, and she knew deep in her heart that this was an encounter like no other. Despite her shock, despite the havoc He wreaked in her life, Mary embraced her Father's promise and this new purpose for living with every fiber of her being. "Oh, how my soul praises the Lord. How my spirit rejoices in God my Savior!" (Luke 1:46–47 NLT). Interestingly, throughout the Gospels, Jesus never uses the phrase, "I promise." Why? Because He is the promise. . .for Mary, for you, for a thousand generations. Take a moment right now to quiet your soul and praise Him for being the peace-bringing, life-changing, everlasting promise.

"Be strong and courageous. Do not be afraid or terrified because of them, for the LORD your God goes with you; he will never leave you nor forsake you."
DEUTERONOMY 31:6 NIV

An infinite God can give all of Himself to each of His children. He does not distribute Himself that each may have a part, but to each one He gives all of Himself as fully as if there were no others.
A. W. TOZER

Jesus, You are the promise, the One spoken of for generations, the One who cleanses us from our sins, brings us to the throne, and makes us righteous before the Father. How I rejoice in You—I am bursting with song. Thank You for life that brings so much promise. Amen.

Words of Peace

"I have told you these things, so that in me you may have peace. In this world you will have trouble. But take heart! I have overcome the world."
JOHN 16:33 NIV

As the final days of Jesus' life drew near, the disciples must have been beside themselves with worry. They tried to understand what was about to happen, but could they really? It was so difficult to wrap their brains around all that Jesus was saying. They were confused, overwhelmed, overcome with fear about the future. And Jesus didn't shy away from the truth—things were about to get tough— almost unbearably so. But, just when all hope seemed to be lost, He promised them peace. Can you hear His gentle voice, the words trickling down the disciples' hearts, settling deep into their souls? "Yes, you will have trouble," Jesus said, "but you will also have peace! I have already overcome, there's nothing to fear."

The peace of Jesus is difficult, if not impossible to explain, but it is yours for the taking. May His peace reside deep within your soul.

Words of Sanctification

"But the Advocate, the Holy Spirit. . .will teach you all things and will remind you of everything I have said to you."
JOHN 14:26 NIV

For three years, Jesus was with them, teaching, modeling, leading. The disciples were both confused and amazed by this man who taught them how to live. Now He was leaving. Repeatedly He said to be like Him, but without Him near, how would they do this? How would they remember? How would they carry on His ministry without His presence?

In place of His physical presence, Jesus left the disciples—and us—the marvelous gift of the Holy Spirit. Through the power of the Spirit, the disciples would be made more like their beloved Master. Over time, they would be molded and shaped into the men He created them to be. Sanctification. This process begins with the truth of God, opening our eyes to our former way of life, then offers what Jesus did—an entirely new perspective on ancient truths established at the beginning of time. The Holy Spirit is the gift that keeps on giving, providing the daily guidance, the conviction, and the gentle nudging that guides us on a Christlike path.

"If you love me, keep my commands. And I will ask the Father, and he will give you another advocate to help you and be with you forever—the Spirit of truth. The world cannot accept him, because it neither sees him nor knows him. But you know him, for he lives with you and will be in you."
JOHN 14:15–17 NIV

Nobody ever outgrows scripture;
the Book widens and deepens with our years.
CHARLES H. SPURGEON

Father, I long to be made holy, and to be molded into the likeness of Your Son. I want to see the world through His eyes, and not my own. Help me to be cooperative with the process of sanctification so that I am made more like You. Amen.

Words of Compassion

When the Lord saw her, his heart overflowed
with compassion. "Don't cry!" he said.
LUKE 7:13 NLT

Not only had she lost her only son, she was a widow, never more
alone in her entire life. The grief must have been unbearable, as her
friends held her up, willing her to move, to attend to her son's burial.
When Jesus came upon the scene, His heart broke. He certainly
wasn't obligated to bring the widow's son back to life, but He acted
out of a heart filled with compassion. How He longed to hold her,
to tell her that this life is temporary. If only He could soothe her
wounds for just a moment. So He gave her the one thing He knew
would heal her breaking heart—He gave her back her son.

Jesus' heart of compassion moved Him to heal the sick, to raise
the dead, to give sight to the blind and music to those who could
not hear. Jesus' compassion enabled Him to serve others in ways that
changed them completely.

How can your heart of compassion move you to touch others
with His love?

The Gospel Call

Jesus replied, "Anyone who drinks this water will soon become thirsty again. But those who drink the water I give will never be thirsty again. It becomes a fresh, bubbling spring within them, giving them eternal life."
JOHN 4:13−14 NLT

She was no doubt thirsty, perhaps literally, but she knew, and He knew. The relief she sought would not be found at the bottom of a well. There was an emptiness in her soul, an ache that could not be soothed. But she tried. She numbed her pain in the arms of one man after another, divorcing them, finally giving up marriage entirely. She would just get thirsty again.

Then she encountered the One of her dreams. Of course she didn't know it at first. But this wise man, who knew everything about her, was the One she'd been longing for, whose arms would never tire of her, who would never discard her. He would hold her for eternity. She would never thirst again. "Could it be?" she asked, her heart afraid to believe it was true. "Could this man *really* be the Messiah?" The woman at the well responded to the call of the Gospel, and then she did what we can do: she ran and told everyone the marvelous news.

Jesus told them, "This is the only work God wants from you:
Believe in the one he has sent."
JOHN 6:29 NLT

I cannot make myself right with God, I cannot make my
life perfect; I can only be right with God if I accept the
atonement of the Lord Jesus Christ as an absolute gift.
OSWALD CHAMBERS

Jesus, thank You for the good news of the Gospel. Thank You
for its simplicity, its relevance, and for the joy it brings. Teach me
to share it with others in a way that is honest, meaningful, and true.
Help me to burst with it, a secret too good not to share. Amen.

Words of Wisdom

"The Son of Man came eating and drinking, and they say,
'Here is a glutton and a drunkard, a friend of tax collectors
and sinners.' But wisdom is proved right by her deeds."
MATTHEW 11:19 NIV

There is a difference between knowledge and wisdom. Knowledge is attained. Wisdom is acquired. Knowledge is about amassing facts and details. Wisdom knows the facts, but is more concerned about the big picture, knowing when to apply the facts to the appropriate context. Jesus constantly challenged His listeners to see the big picture. To consider the knowledge they'd gained in a completely different light, to learn to apply it appropriately, to understand the spirit, not just the letter of the law.

For us, this doesn't happen overnight, nor does it come naturally. Wisdom is acquired by years of practice, learning from others, opening hearts and minds to the teaching of Jesus, and learning to apply it appropriately through the guidance of the Holy Spirit.

Words of Light

When Jesus spoke again to the people, he said,
"I am the light of the world. Whoever follows me will
never walk in darkness, but will have the light of life."
JOHN 8:12 NIV

The Good News is portrayed beautifully in John 8:12. Jesus is the Light, and He promises the light of life to all who follow Him. Jesus possessed two qualities that enabled Him to share this message without wavering. The first was complete confidence in His identity and His purpose. He was the Light, the Son of God, whether others acknowledged Him or not, and His purpose was clear: To do the will of the One who sent Him (John 6:38). Additionally, He had no interest in being a people pleaser, nor did He have a need to tell them what they wanted to hear. His unswerving commitment was to His Father, and this was the driving force behind every word He spoke. The Good News of the Gospel naturally flowed out of this commitment.

The natural response to receiving the light is to share it with others. When you are completely confident in your identity in Christ, your life purpose becomes clear and you are free from the temptation to be a people pleaser. This dark world is desperate for the Light.

The Hope of Heaven

"My Father's house has many rooms; if that were not so, would I
have told you that I am going there to prepare a place for you? And if
I go and prepare a place for you, I will come back and take you
to be with me that you also may be where I am."
JOHN 14:2—3 NIV

It is their last night together. The atmosphere is charged with
electricity, mystery. The words Jesus speaks this night are all at once
terrifying and exhilarating. There is fear, there is peace. Then a
promise: I am going to prepare a place for you. I will come for you
and take you where I am. The One who was at the creation of the
world has now promised to create a new home for His loved ones.
Can you imagine, as you gaze upon the beauty and majesty of earthly
creation, what heaven must be like? If the Creator invested so much
time and detail in the glory of the Grand Canyon, and the intricacies
of a hummingbird, how much more marvelous must heaven be? It is
beyond our mind's ability to comprehend. But we have the promise,
spoken by the Word. He prepares a place for us and we will be with
Him for Life. Everlasting, eternal, glorious life.

Praise be to the God and Father of our Lord Jesus Christ! In his great mercy he has given us new birth into a living hope through the resurrection of Jesus Christ from the dead, and into an inheritance that can never perish, spoil or fade. This inheritance is kept in heaven for you.
1 PETER 1:3–4 NIV

I've read the last page of the Bible.
It's all going to turn out all right.
BILLY GRAHAM

My Father in heaven, I have an inheritance! In a world where thieves and moths and rust destroy, when seemingly precious things are so cheap and temporary, I am thrilled beyond measure at the thought of an inheritance reserved for me. Thank You for this marvelous promise. Amen.

What a Friend We Have in Jesus

What a friend we have in Jesus, all our sins and griefs to bear!
What a privilege to carry everything to God in prayer!
O what peace we often forfeit, O what needless pain we bear,
All because we do not carry everything to God in prayer.

Have we trials and temptations? Is there trouble anywhere?
We should never be discouraged; take it to the Lord in prayer.
Can we find a friend so faithful who will all our sorrows share?
Jesus knows our every weakness; take it to the Lord in prayer.

Are we weak and heavy laden, cumbered with a load of care?
Precious Savior, still our refuge, take it to the Lord in prayer.
Do your friends despise, forsake you? Take it to the Lord in prayer!
In His arms He'll take and shield you; you will find a solace there.

Blessed Savior, Thou hast promised Thou wilt all our burdens bear.
May we ever, Lord, be bringing all to Thee in earnest prayer.
Soon in glory bright unclouded there will be no need for prayer;
Rapture, praise, and endless worship will be our sweet portion there.

JOSEPH M. SCRIVEN, 1855

Born in Ireland in 1819, Joseph M. Scriven moved to Canada to begin a new life after his fiancée died in a tragic drowning accident the day before their wedding. While working as a teacher, he fell in love again, but his dreams were shattered once more when his fiancée died of an illness before they could marry. In his brokenness and grief, he found great comfort in the Lord. Around the time of his fiancée's death he received word that his mother was ill. Unable to go to her, he penned the words to "What a Friend We Have in Jesus" and sent them to comfort her.

Almost thirty years later his poem was discovered by a friend and published in a book called *Hymns and Other Verses*. Composer Charles C. Converse put the words to music, and Ira D. Sankey, D. L. Moody's song leader, included it in his hymn book, *Sankey's Gospel Hymns Number 1*. Out of one man's intense grief came a song that has touched countless lives.

What a Friend!

"Greater love has no one than this:
to lay down one's life for one's friends."
JOHN 15:13 NIV

When Jesus died on the cross, He died once and for all. He willingly laid down His life for mankind. Certainly other men have died in order to save the life of another. Soldiers in battle, firefighters, and other first responders to tragedies. But Christ chose His death. He died to fulfill the requirement of the sacrifice of a lamb. His blood was graciously shed to atone for our sins. He left the glory of heaven in order to come to earth and experience life as a man. Fully God and yet fully man, He went to the cross and offered up His perfect life so that sinners might have abundant and eternal life. He did not die for the righteous but for the unrighteous. His death and resurrection is the bridge for us to commune with our holy God.

And so, in the midst of great joy and on your darkest day, remember that you have a friend in Jesus. He is the best friend you could ever ask for, faithful and loving to the end. He bore every sin you have ever and will ever commit when He hung on that old rugged cross. And He did not stay in the tomb. Jesus is alive! He sits at the right hand of the Father, and He lives in your heart. He wants to bear your sorrows for you. Call upon the name of Jesus. He is a friend like no other.

The Privilege of Prayer

Rejoice always, pray continually, give thanks in all circumstances;
for this is God's will for you in Christ Jesus.
1 THESSALONIANS 5:16—18 NIV

Prayer is not optional. God calls His children to pray constantly, in all circumstances—good and bad alike. The believer would be foolish not to accept the gift and exercise the great privilege of prayer. Through Jesus, Christians are able to commune with the God of the universe. Prayer is the avenue through which we praise the Lord, thank Him, ask Him for specific needs to be met, and lift others up to Him. The Bible tells us to cast our cares on the Lord because He cares for us. How comforting to know that we have a place to turn and someone who is always there, ready to listen and guide.

If you have not been taking advantage of the privilege of prayer, begin today. It is never too late to begin talking with your Father. Start by expressing to God how much you love Him. Thank Him for all that He has done and all that He is going to do. Go before Him boldly, remembering that your words are not bouncing off the ceiling but being heard by your loving heavenly Father. Prayer is a privilege that is granted to every single believer in Jesus Christ. Pray in the powerful name of Jesus and watch as your prayers are answered.

This is the confidence we have in approaching God: that if we ask anything according to his will, he hears us. And if we know that he hears us— whatever we ask—we know that we have what we asked of him.
1 JOHN 5:14—15 NIV

We have to pray with our eyes on God,
not on the difficulties.
OSWALD CHAMBERS

Why is it so hard for me to pray, Lord? My mind
wanders, and sometimes I wonder if You even hear my
words. Father, I want to be faithful in prayer. I know
that intimate fellowship only comes as a result of time spent
together. Create in me a desire to pray and remind me of
the wonderful privilege I have been given that I might
converse with the God of the universe! Amen.

Forfeited Peace

For to set the mind on the flesh is death,
but to set the mind on the Spirit is life and peace.
ROMANS 8:6 ESV

Every elementary school student learns about opposites. Hot and cold. Up and down. Light versus dark. But have you considered the opposite of peace? Who wants to live a life filled with turmoil and anxiety? Imagine the ocean in all of its might crashing in upon the shore again and again as a wild tropical storm devours a row of pristine beach houses. The wind howls all around you. You try to run but it knocks you to your knees. The pelting rain blinds you. Your heart pounds within your chest as you cling to life, hoping only to survive. *Turmoil.* Now force your mind to dwell on the opposite. Gentle waves lap at the shore. A gulf breeze blows. You walk in silence along the coastline, dipping your toes in the cool water, turning your face to the warmth of the sun. *Peace.*

Each day you make a choice between the calm and the storm, between—as scripture declares—life and death. Do you set your mind on the things of this world? Are you so caught up in work or relationships that you have squeezed God out of your heart? So many Christians forfeit the peace God intends for them to possess. Focus on the Holy Spirit. He is your comforter and counselor. Jesus asked the Father to send Him to you that you might live a life of peace, not distress. Make a conscious choice today to set your mind on the Spirit. Peace is just a prayer away.

Trials and Temptations

No temptation has overtaken you except what is common to mankind. And God is faithful; he will not let you be tempted beyond what you can bear. But when you are tempted, he will also provide a way out so that you can endure it.
1 CORINTHIANS 10:13 NIV

Life is a maze. Trying to find your way around the corners and avoiding bumping into dead ends can be quite the challenge! Do you find yourself hitting the same wall again and again in life? Are you continuously tempted to travel in a direction that you know is not God's best? Is there a trial that weighs on you, holding you back from the freedom you once knew in Christ? God is still there. He is faithful to His children. He will never give you more than you can bear. If there is a great struggle in your life, God knows you will be able to overcome. It will take time and constant surrender to the Lord, but you will get beyond it. If there are temptations that nip at your ankles, demanding your attention, be done with them! Give them to God. You may have to pray daily to receive the strength to resist them. Hourly even. But God stands ready to save you. He desires that none of His children should give in to the clever traps of Satan.

Life is a maze. That is certain. But God offers you a hand to hold as you navigate its twists and turns. Ask Him for help. He is waiting to see if you are willing to accept it. He knows how to get you from point A to point B. Let God show you the way out.

Consider it pure joy, my brothers and sisters, whenever you face trials of many kinds, because you know that the testing of your faith produces perseverance. Let perseverance finish its work so that you may be mature and complete, not lacking anything.
JAMES 1:2–4 NIV

What would you expect? Sin will not come to you, saying, "I am sin." It would do little harm if it did. Sin always seems "good, and pleasant, and desirable," at the time of commission.
JAMES CHARLES RYLE

This one particular trial almost has me beat, God. I am just not strong enough. It is too difficult to face, too powerful to conquer, too sad to endure. But You, O Lord, are stronger than even my greatest struggle. It is not too hard for You. You are a mighty warrior ready to go to battle for my soul. And yet, You also wipe away my tears with a gentle hand. Lord, I need You so. Amen.

Trouble in This Life

Behold, I am doing a new thing;
now it springs forth, do you not perceive it?
I will make a way in the wilderness
and rivers in the desert.
ISAIAH 43:19 ESV

Solomon, one of the wisest men who ever lived, concludes in the book of Ecclesiastes that life is hard. He finds it all meaningless, in fact. Every generation will experience loss, disappointment, and trials. Ever since Adam and Eve tasted of the forbidden fruit in Eden, this world has been less than perfect. So, it's a given. We live and breathe and make our way in a fallen world every moment from birth until the last breath we take in these shells. Sounds like bad news, doesn't it? But there is always good news with Jesus!

The Bible declares that in Christ we are more than conquerors. It proclaims that in Him we can do all things. The words of the holy scriptures advise us not to worry about the troubles we will face in the future but to let each day unfold in its own time. Trust God. He is doing a new thing in your life! He is making a way through the trouble to the other side. Did He not prove that He is able when He parted the Red Sea and allowed His children to cross it? The Egyptians were caught up in the waters and drowned just as the last Israelite planted his foot on the safe shoreline. Face the inevitable troubles of this life with your sovereign God.

Be Encouraged!

*"The LORD himself goes before you and will be with you;
he will never leave you nor forsake you. Do not be afraid;
do not be discouraged."*
DEUTERONOMY 31:8 NIV

Do not be afraid. Do not be dismayed. Do not be discouraged. These words
appear regularly in the Bible. Often they were spoken before soldiers
went into battle as a reminder that God was going ahead of them
and they had nothing to fear in their enemies. Every day as believers,
we fight a spiritual battle against the prince of this world, Satan.
These words are not suggestions. They are *commands.* And yet many
Christians find themselves stuck deep down in the mire of fear and
discouragement. What causes followers of Christ to lose sight of the
fact that God has it all under control? Could it be that they forget to
take their worries to the Lord in prayer?

Remember running to a parent or grandparent when you were
a child? If you had good news to share, you wanted to get to that
person as quickly as possible in order to share it. If you were hurt or
sad, you could hardly wait to be wrapped up in a safe embrace. This
is how it should be between you and your heavenly Father. Whatever
is troubling you today, wait no longer to run to Him. Do not be
discouraged! He is a great big God and you only need to make your
way into His loving arms to remember that He is the source of all joy
and encouragement.

The name of the LORD is a strong tower;
the righteous run to it and are safe.
PROVERBS 18:10 NIV

I would go to the deeps a hundred times to cheer a downcast
spirit. It is good for me to have been afflicted, that I might
know how to speak a word in season to one that is weary.
CHARLES SPURGEON

Lord, encourage my heart today as only You can do. I need
to sense that I am deeply loved. The worries and pressures of
the world could easily discourage were it not for the intimate
fellowship I share with You. No matter what comes my way,
You will be steadfast and true. With You on my side,
nothing can overtake me or steal my joy. Thank You, Lord,
for loving me the way that You do. Amen.

Faithful Friend

But the Lord is faithful. He will establish
you and guard you against the evil one.
2 THESSALONIANS 3:3 ESV

A faithful friend. How could I ask for more? You are incapable of faithlessness. You are God—all-powerful and all too aware of my sin. . .and yet, You remain loyal to me through it all.

My life is a roller-coaster ride. In my humanity, emotions take me up and down. It is a wild adventure! And yet, after I twist and turn and do a few loop-the-loops, I find You there. You stand steady and true at the gate, waiting. I get off the coaster for a rest between rides. You take my hand. We walk for a while. You remind me that I am Your child and You are my Father, this life on earth is temporary, and these trials shall pass just as the last ones did.

Alas, another ride is inevitable. You help me buckle my seat belt. And You do an amazing thing! You take the seat beside me. We ride together. I scream for joy. . .and then from sheer terror. Life is funny that way. Up and down we go, faster, faster. . .I look to You. You are not screaming or afraid. You are not thrown off balance or shaken. You know it all comes out okay in the end. I take Your hand and squeeze it hard. You don't seem to mind. Thank You, Lord, for riding with me, for holding me steady, for being faithful. Your love amazes me.

He Knows Your Weaknesses

*A final word: Be strong in the
Lord and in his mighty power.*
EPHESIANS 6:10 NLT

From prison, the apostle Paul wrote to the church at Ephesus instructing the people on how to live God-honoring lives. The letter is packed with insights including teaching on salvation by grace through faith in Christ alone. As Paul concluded this important letter, which some scholars believe was distributed to several early churches, he chose these words:

"Finally, be strong in the Lord and in His mighty power."

The famous reference to the "full armor of God" comes next. Paul warns that the believers' fight is not against this world but rather against evil spiritual forces of the heavenly realm.

Paul was aware that the early Christians were weak. He himself was weak. His only "super power" came directly from God. Paul knew from whom his strength came and he carefully laid out the necessities for the Ephesians to tap into this same strength. The *belt of truth, breastplate of righteousness, feet fitted with the gospel of peace, shield of faith, helmet of salvation, and sword of the Spirit* were—and are—essentials! Christians today should heed Paul's advice. God has provided us with His Word and with the privilege of prayer. We are weak, but in Jesus we are strong!

Next time you part ways with a fellow Christian, consider admonishing him or her in the way Paul did the Ephesians. Encourage your friend to *"Be strong in the Lord!"*

But he said to me, "My grace is sufficient for you, for my power is made perfect in weakness." Therefore I will boast all the more gladly of my weaknesses, so that the power of Christ may rest upon me.
2 CORINTHIANS 12:9 ESV

Many a humble soul will be amazed to find that the seed that is sowed in weakness, in the dust of daily life, has blossomed into immortal flowers under the eye of the Lord.
HARRIET BEECHER STOWE

Lord Jesus, I am weak but You are strong. I sang the song as a little child and how true I have learned it is! I gain strength to persevere through my relationship with You. How do non-believers make it in this life? They must be so depleted of energy and joy at all times. I am blessed to be replenished daily with a dose of my Savior's strength! Thank You, Jesus, for strengthening me.

Refuge in Christ

So God has given both his promise and his oath. These two things are unchangeable because it is impossible for God to lie. Therefore, we who have fled to him for refuge can have great confidence as we hold to the hope that lies before us. This hope is a strong and trustworthy anchor for our souls. It leads us through the curtain into God's inner sanctuary.
HEBREWS 6:18–19 NLT

A curtain separated man from the holiest part of the temple. When Jesus took His last breath on the cross and submitted His spirit to the Father, the curtain was torn. It was torn from top to bottom. Everything changed in that instant.

Sinners may enter into the presence of Almighty God through the blood of Jesus, the perfect sacrifice. He gives us access to our holy God. Without Him, we would be separated from God.

Stand firm in this life. Cling to God through your faith in Christ. Recognize your salvation as a wonderful refuge from this dark and dangerous world. Like a boat at sea held steady by an anchor, you are anchored in Christ. He is a strong anchor. Otherwise, certainly the strong winds would carry you away. The prince of this world is a dark being. Satan would love nothing more than to see you tossing and turning upon the waves of life, adrift from the shore with no port, no home, no haven in which to rest. But you do not belong to this world. Nor do you belong to the evil one. Your hope is found in nothing less than the blood of the Son of the Most High. Make Jesus your refuge. Ask Him to protect you and to hold you close. He is the only true security.

Forsaken by Others

"As for you, you meant evil against me, but God meant it for good in order to bring about this present result, to preserve many people alive."
GENESIS 50:20 NASB

Joseph understood being forsaken by others. His own brothers sold him into slavery. They were jealous and wanted him out of their lives. But that is not how the story ends. . . .

Joseph wound up in Egypt and thus a fascinating turn of events crafted by the providential hand of God began. Joseph became the personal attendant of Potiphar, a very important official of Pharaoh, the ruler of Egypt. He then spent years in prison for a crime he did not commit when Potiphar's wife told awful lies about him. But eventually Joseph was released, finding favor with Pharaoh by interpreting his dreams.

Joseph, who was once sold into slavery on the side of the road, landed the position of prime minister of Egypt!

When Joseph's brothers appeared before him again years later, they didn't recognize him. There was a great famine in Israel. Their father, Jacob, sent them to buy grain in Egypt. After a test, Joseph determined that his brothers' cold hearts had changed. They feared him when he said, "I am Joseph." But they had nothing to fear. Joseph forgave them. He told them to gather all their relatives and come to Egypt where he provided land. God used Joseph to save the nation of Israel from which the Messiah would come. What others meant for evil, God used for good.

When others forsake you, look to God. He will always be with you, and He will use even the deepest hurts in your life for good.

Rescue me from the mud;
don't let me sink any deeper!
Save me from those who hate me,
and pull me from these deep waters.
Don't let the floods overwhelm me,
or the deep waters swallow me,
or the pit of death devour me.
PSALM 69:14–15 NLT

If you live for any joy on earth, you may be forsaken;
but, oh, live for Jesus, and he will never forsake you!
MATTHEW SIMPSON

Other people let me down, Father. I know that I let them down
as well. It is part of being human! But You are faithful even
when my friends turn away. Sometimes I go through my list of
friends and it seems no one wants to spend time with me.
I become discouraged. But then I remember that You are always
there. You are my most faithful friend. I love You, Lord.

Shield and Solace

Blessed be the God and Father of our Lord Jesus Christ, the Father
of mercies and God of all comfort, who comforts us in all our tribulation,
that we may be able to comfort those who are in any trouble, with
the comfort with which we ourselves are comforted by God.
2 CORINTHIANS 1:3–4 NKJV

"God does not comfort us to make us comfortable only, but to make us comforters," Dr. John Henry J. H. Jowett once said. He was an English pastor who served also as pastor of a New York church. People lined up to hear his sermons regardless of the fact that he read aloud as he preached. Why? It was because the truths were biblical and right on target.

This is one of those truths: God comforts us so that we might comfort others. Dr. Jowett did not create it. He taught it directly from the Bible.

Once you have known the comfort of God, you will want to pass it on. When the Lord Himself has carried you through a dark and frightening trial and you reach the other side, you will never miss an opportunity to comfort someone facing a similar struggle. If you have experienced the loss of a parent, a child, or a marriage, look around for those who are in the same boat. If you have been comforted when you lost your way and had to make your way back to God, it won't be hard to find another soul battling the same sin or addiction. God comforts that we might comfort others. If you have found solace in the loving arms of the Lord, lead another to those same safe arms. Go therefore into your hurting world and. . .pass it on.

The Savior's Promise

Praise be to the Lord, to God our Savior,
who daily bears our burdens.
PSALM 68:19 NIV

Jesus promises to bear our burdens. What kind of friend does that? Certainly some friends will walk alongside us, but none except Jesus is able to take our burden from us. He calls to you and asks you to lay down your heavy load. He says to cast your cares upon Him because He is strong and He can handle all your worries. He cares for you. He declares that nothing will be able to snatch you out of the Father's hand. Nothing. Not angels or demons. Not anything past, present, or future. Once you are saved by the blood of Jesus, it covers you, gives you a new name, and secures your position before Almighty God. You are righteous through that blood. You are God's beloved child, adopted through grace and unconditionally loved.

So why worry and fret? Why grow anxious about your current situation or needlessly stay up at night contemplating an unknown future? Run to Christ. He is ready and willing to take all of your burdens upon Himself. He is not just the classmate who offers to carry your books or backpack for a while. Eventually, the classmate returns the load. Not so with Jesus! He is the Son of the Living God. He wants to cast those burdens as far as the east is from the west and replace them with peace and joy and contentment. He is your blessed Messiah. He wants to see you laugh and rejoice again. Give it all to Jesus. And don't look back.

We are hard-pressed on every side, yet not crushed;
we are perplexed, but not in despair; persecuted,
but not forsaken; struck down, but not destroyed.
2 CORINTHIANS 4:8–9 NKJV

When an answer I did not expect comes to a prayer which
I believed I truly meant, I shrink back from it; if the burden
my Lord asks me to bear be not the burden of my heart's
choice, and I fret inwardly and do not welcome His will,
then I know nothing of Calvary love.
AMY CARMICHAEL

Oh Jesus, You say that You will gladly bear my burdens
for me. But so often I resist Your offer. I stay up all night
worrying about the future when my future is secure in You.
I worry about tomorrow when, as the Bible says, it has enough
trouble of its own. I want to surrender my cares to You.
Take them, Jesus. Help me to surrender, I ask.
Help me to trust You. Amen.

Earnest Prayer

You, God, are my God, earnestly I seek you;
I thirst for you, my whole being longs for you,
in a dry and parched land where there is no water.
PSALM 63:1 NIV

Earnest prayers. They fill the pages of the Bible. Jonah prayed from the belly of the great fish. Hannah cried out in anguish for a child. Elijah, wanting to prove the strength of the one true God, prayed for fire. David prayed for forgiveness when he had committed adultery. Jesus, the very Son of God, prayed so furiously in the Garden of Gethsemane that His sweat turned to blood. Have you prayed earnestly to the Lord for a need in your life? Prayer is the way that you make known to God what you need and desire.

God does not always answer prayers the way we think He should. But He is faithful to answer the prayers of His children. Sometimes the answer is yes. Other times it is no. The Father may answer your prayer now. He may require you to wait for some of your prayers to be answered.

Imagine walking through a desert. You have no water and the sun beats down on you, draining you of all strength. Suddenly you see a lush waterfall pouring into a glistening lake. Wouldn't you run to it and quench your thirst? Certainly you would not only drink from it but plunge into the water, refreshing your weary body. Seek your heavenly Father in prayer in this same manner. Seek Him earnestly. He will refresh your spirit.

No Need for Prayer in Glory

"He will wipe every tear from their eyes. There will be no more death or mourning or crying or pain, for the old order of things has passed away."
REVELATION 21:4 NIV

Prayer is for the here and now. It is an avenue of direct communication with the Father through faith in Christ. While it is a beautiful thing, there will be no need for prayer in heaven. The Bible tells us that we see only a dim reflection here on earth, but in heaven we shall see fully even as we are fully known by God.

On this earth, we have longings. We have unmet desires. We think we need a lot of things. Really, we only need God. One day, when we are in His glorious kingdom, we will understand. We won't need to carry our burdens to Jesus any longer. There will be no more burdens. We won't cry any more tears. The Word of God declares that there will be no tears in heaven. How can it be that there will be no more grief? There will be no more grief because there will be no more death. Pain will not exist. You will have a new body. Imagine it! You know those little aches? You know those parts of your earthly body that don't work quite right? They will trouble you no longer. You will have a spiritual body. While heaven remains a mystery, we know that Jesus says it will be joyous there. Eternal happiness. So pray while you are here on this earth. Walk with God through prayer. One day you will see your Father face-to-face!

Jesus, Your Forever Friend

But in him it is always Yes. For all the promises of God find their Yes in him. That is why it is through him that we utter our Amen to God for his glory.
2 CORINTHIANS 1:19–20 ESV

When a Southerner visits New York City, she often hears the phrase, "You're not from here, are you?" The slowness of a Southern drawl is evidence that the Big Apple is not her home! Similarly, Earth is not our home. We are just passing through. Heaven is our home and we are heaven-bound.

The important things will last. The rest will not. Most of the things of earth are not lasting. Just the relationships. Just your walk with Jesus. He is eternal. Jesus of Nazareth is the same Jesus we find praying earnestly in the Garden of Gethsemane. He is the same Jesus who healed the sick and raised the dead to life in the years in between. And when the Father did not remove the cup, Jesus grasped it with all His might and drank deep of it. . .for all mankind. And as the rich, red blood of perfect sacrifice ran down His face, it saved us.

So what will you do with Jesus? Your answer is crucial. Choose to follow Christ. Let Him lead you down every path. Ask Him which way to turn at each crossroad. When He says to stop, stop. When He blesses the journey, run freely into it. Jesus never falters. He will never come up short or leave you stranded. He knows the way because He *is* the Way. He is a truer friend than any you will ever know on earth. As you wait for His sure return, keep singing: *"What a friend we have in Jesus. . . ."*

Now may the God of peace who brought up our Lord Jesus from the dead, that great Shepherd of the sheep, through the blood of the everlasting covenant, make you complete in every good work to do His will, working in you what is well pleasing in His sight, through Jesus Christ, to whom be glory forever and ever. Amen.
HEBREWS 13:20–21 NKJV

Radical obedience to Christ is not easy. . . It's not comfort, not health, not wealth, and not prosperity in this world. Radical obedience to Christ risks losing all these things. But in the end, such risk finds its reward in Christ. And he is more than enough for us.
DAVID PLATT

Lord, one day I will praise You day and night. For eternity I will worship You with the angels and all the saints who have gone before me. My portion will be sweet. On my lips there will always be a song declaring Your greatness. Let me taste of heaven on this earth. Find me utterly surrendered to You when I sing. Remove the distractions of this world. May my focus be on You, Jesus.

Scripture Index

Contributors

"To God Be the Glory": Gale Hyatt

"Amazing Grace": Jennifer Hahn

"It Is Well with My Soul": Darlene Franklin

"All Things Bright and Beautiful": Emily Biggers

"Blessed Assurance": Shanna D. Gregor

"Sweet Hour of Prayer": Donna K. Maltese

"Count Your Blessing": MariLee Parrish

"Great Is Thy Faithfulness": JoAnne Simmons

"What a Friend We Have in Jesus": Emily Biggers

"Wonderful Words of Life": Joanna Bloss

Compilation and hymn writer biographies by Jill Jones